Being Faithful in Diversity

Gary D Bouma

Adelaide
2011

Being Faithful in Diversity:

Religions and Social Policy in Multifaith Socities

The Llyod Geering Lectures 2010

Gary D Bouma

National Library of Australia Cataloguing-in-Publication entry: (pbk)

Author: Bouma, Gary D.

Title: Being faithful in diversity : religion and social policy in
           multifaith societies / Gary D Bouma.

ISBN: 9781921511028 (pbk.)

Notes: Includes bibliographical references and index.

Subjects: Religious pluralism.
          Religion and sociology.
          Religions.

Dewey Number: 201.5

Cover design by Astrid Sengkey
All original photos taken from PWR 2009

An imprint of the ATF Ltd
PO Box 504
Hindmarsh, SA 5007
ABN 90 116 359 963
www.atfpress.com

Table of Contents

Acknowledgments   ix
Preface: Sir Lloyd Geering   xi
Introduction   xiii

Chapter One
The Rise and Consequences of Religious Diversity   **1**

An Old Normal: Fear of Diversity   1
The Passing of the Old Normal   3
The Emergence of Religious Diversity: Some Data   5
The Consequence of Increased Religious Diversity   14
    The re-entry of religious voices into the public sphere   15
    Familiarity with diversity   17
    Increased salience of religious identity   19
Secular Societies   22
Some Further Reading   24

Chapter Two
Responses to Diversity:
Road Rage on the Highway to Heaven   **25**

Dealing with Difference   26
Religious Revitalisation   27
Why Revitalisation   29
Religious Diversity and Religious Rivalry   31
    Competition vs conflict   32
    Negative othering   33
Competitive Piety   36
Diversity and Boundary Marking   38
Real vs Imagined Others   41

The Outcome of Negative Othering   42
Road Rage   43
Conclusion   45
Some Further Reading   46

Chapter Three
**Responses to Diversity—Snapping Along the Spandex—
Diversity and Social Cohesion**   **47**

Defining Social Cohesion   48
Types of Social Cohesion   48
Challenges of Social Cohesion   53
Managing Diversity   54
Factors in the Management of Religious Diversity   56
Some National Examples of Diversity Management   59
Religious Voices in Secular Societies   61
A Case Study: Church Supports Civil Unions for
          Same Sex Couples   64
Strategies of Exclusion   68
Strategies of Inclusion   70
Conclusion   72
Some Further Reading   74

Chapter Four
**Being Faithful in Diversity—
Beyond Exclusivism and Relativism**   **75**

Relating to Those Who are Religiously Different   77
Faithful to What?   78
          Creed   79
          Ritual practice   80
          Religious identity   80
          How things were   80
          Relationship with the numinous   81
Theological Orientations to Difference   82
          Exclusivism   82
          Inclusivism   82
          Supersessionism   83
          Relativism   84
Some Things I Know About Religious Diversity   85
Criteria of Assessment   87

Seeking Objective Standards 88
    Universal values 88
    Sustainability 90
    Consequences 90
    Compassion 93
    Eternal consequences 95
The Problem of Accountability 97
An Alternative to Judging 101
Is Dialogue the Answer? 103
The Perspective of Diversity 104
Some Further Reading 106

Chapter Five

A Way Forward **107**

Index 111

Acknowledgments

This book began as the Lloyd Geering Lectures in Wellington, New Zealand, in 2010. I am deeply grateful to the St Andrew's Trust and to Sir Lloyd Geering for making this possible. Their generosity is greatly appreciated. Thanks also go to Maxine and Jim Cunningham for their hospitality and for proposing that I be invited to give these lectures. At the end Sir Lloyd Geering pointed out that this was the first time that these lectures which are supposed to be in the area of Religion and Society have in fact been given by a sociologist. I am honoured to have had the opportunity to break the ice in this way.

This book has grown out of my decades of work both as a researcher and a facilitator in the area of religious diversity. The support of my colleagues in the Australian Multicultural Foundation, Victorian Multicultural Commission, UNESCO, and The Global Terrorism Research Centre (Monash University) is acknowledged. This book also is an Australian contribution to the University of Ottawa based SSHRC funded Major Collaborative Research Initiatives Program 'Religious Diversity and Its Limits: Moving Beyond Tolerance and Accommodation'.

I would like acknowledge the invaluable support of my wife Patricia who colleague in interfaith activities and sounding board as well as patient partner has in many ways made this possible. She also provided the photographs used in this book.

I would also like to acknowledge the assistance to bring this book to publication from The School of Political and Social Inquiry, Monash University, and to ATF Press.

The chapters in this book were given as originally lectures and so with this publication a more popular, less formal or academic style of presentation has been maintained. I am grateful to the people in Wellington who attended, engaged the issues with challenging questions and warmly responded to the lectures.

Preface

Lloyd Geering

As I write this Preface to *Being Faithful in Diversity* by Gary Bouma of Monash University, Melbourne I observe the fact that in the twenty-seven years of the existence of the society in New Zealand where these lectures were first delivered, a society that has the task of the study of religion and society, so far as I can remember there has never been a sociologist. Now that, when you come to think of it, is pretty odd when we call ourselves The St Andrew's Trust for the Study of Society and Religion. These chapters fill a gap. I wonder if one of the reasons why we have not had a sociologist is that it is a bit like St Augustine when he was talking about time. He said he knew exactly what time was until he started to think about it. Well we all of us think we know what society is until we start to think about it and then we are all at sea, which is one of the reasons why Margaret Thatcher probably said there is no such thing as society. Society is a very difficult concept in many respects.

Of course just as religion, if you are going to discuss it, depends a great deal on how you are going to define it, so too society is a very difficult thing to think about until you try to determine, what is it that makes a society? If 60,000 people gather at a park to see a football match are they a society? There is something that joins them together and they have a common interest in what happens at that game. Of course they are divided on the fact of which side they want to win the game. In these chapters, Gary, you have brought an insight that society may be seeking some kind of future harmony but in doing so it also raises a whole lot of issues which divide it. And what is more, society exists at a whole lot of different levels. Each of the readers of this volume of essays belongs to a variety of different societies and contexts. We are part of a particular human society but we are also part of one in our own particular interests.

Gary, you are particularly concerned with the role that religion might play in society. The question must be asked, 'does religion join a society together or does it divide societies one from another?' It is interesting to observe that two of the great religious traditions, Christianity and Islam, both set out in the hope of producing a completely, total, harmonious human society. Mohammad called it the brotherhood of people. It was the brotherhood of human kind that he set out to produce. Christians of course took over from the Jews who were already making their converts. That they should go out making converts was odd, but nevertheless the Christians took it over hoping that in fact it would bring all people together into one harmonious society. Well, it is clear from history, we have not managed a harmonious society well and indeed today human society is more divided than it has ever been before in human history.

Gary, your chapters have raised so many questions, without all too many answers of course, but you have raised all sorts of questions that society faces us with today. To attempt in today's society to do our little bit to bring some kind of harmony, good will, compassion that will draw people together is in fact a very big demand. So we are grateful to you for the way in which you have shown so lucidly the complexity of the situation.

Lloyd Geering
New Zealand

Introduction

Religious diversity is my interest and has been my professional commitment for about forty years. It is interesting to me that it has become a little bit more interesting toward the end than it was at the beginning, when people, like my PhD thesis advisor said 'why bother Bouma, there is not going to be any religion by the end of the twentieth century'. We know them to be wrong now. I was able to discuss this with my thesis advisor before he died and have a good chuckle about it.

Religious diversity is probably one of the most important changes affecting our lives in the twenty-first century. Yes, those changes began earlier, but the twenty-first century is going to be about the management of religious diversity, doing it well, or getting it terribly wrong. Religious diversity has increased and become a part of daily life, in a way that it probably never was before, or if it was, it was much more isolated than it is now. It has become the new normal in the lives of most people. This book examines religious diversity and how it is that we cope with religious diversity, both locally and globally. The first chapter, 'The Rise And Consequences Of Religious Diversity', focuses on some facts about religious diversity. The second chapter, 'Responses to Diversity: Road Rage on the Highway to Heaven' examines some of the hostile and negative reactions to religious diversity. Chapter three, 'Responses to Diversity: Snapping along the Spandex: Diversity and Social Cohesion', discusses ways that religious diversity stretches the social fabric this way and that and how social cohesion is possible under conditions of diversity. In the fourth chapter, 'Being Faithful in Diversity: Beyond Relativism and Exclusivity', we come to the fundamental issue of is it all just about relativism or are there some criteria that are emerging by which we can distinguish healthy from unhealthy religions. If religions are not all the same, and they are not, then are there limits, standards and criteria to which religions can be held accountable. Finally, in chapter five, 'A Way Forward', points to some challenges. That is the journey that I hope to take you on in this book and you will join me, I hope, in having some fun in doing this thinking about the issues as we go along.

What is religion and spirituality? Well religions and spiritualities both relate to dimensions of human life that intersect with and point beyond the now, the ordinary and the material. Religion includes beliefs and practices about questions like: Is this all there is? Why get out of bed in the morning? What is it all about? And along with the answers and practices come communities and histories and identities, a sense of belonging, rights, celebrations that both connect the now with the more than, the other than. Some people make a huge difference between religion and spirituality. I say religion without spirituality is as dead as a doornail. And spirituality without religion, well, you can not do something more than three times without it becoming organised anyway, and so you are not going to have much spirituality that you can detect, that is not already well on its way to becoming a religion. This is a sensitising definition to help us detect religion even if it is not found in the containers we are accustomed to.

The focus of this book is on Australia and New Zealand with some reference to Canada. These former British colonies share much and yet are quite distinct in the ways they manage religious diversity. For a richer comparison of the ways nations manage religious diversity I recommend *Religious Diversity in Southeast Asia and the Pacific Islands.*[1] The examples will be drawn largely from Australia and New Zealand. The ways these issues have emerged in Europe is so fundamentally different as to require a major work just to provide the background necessary to any comparison. The United States is different again. The facile transposition of issues and the application of responses from Europe or the USA are misguided at best and quite frankly dangerous. Thus the target audience is primarily Australians and New Zealanders, and particularly those of faith.

While much of what I say will be directed at a Christian audience as the lectures were presented in that context, the issues raised and the questions to be faced are the same for all religious groups. Diversity challenges everyone and every perspective and faith, each spirituality and religion. How to respond to diversity, how to be faithful to self, other, religion and spirituality are challenges to all thoughtful people. Given that I am a person of faith, a Christian, these issues confront me in ways I cannot dodge or dismiss but this fact also makes me sensitive to the issues faced by others of faith and for that matter those who believe there is nothing.

While you will learn more about me as the book unfolds, some preliminary information may be of help. I am a priest and sociologist and have been all my life. My father was a Professor of Sociology and preached occasionally. Theology was a sport played fiercely on Sunday afternoons—there was little else that was allowed—when gathered at my grandparents' home we would deconstruct at least three sermons, discuss current events and issues arising from church and society relationships. Religious diversity was seen by my father's side of the family as a disease to be overcome by active proselytising and mission work. However, religious diversity was built into my family, as my mother's family did not go to church. Moreover they were the loving, caring and affectionate ones.

Some Further Reading

1. Gary Bouma, Rod Ling and Doug Pratt *Religious Diversity in Southeast Asia and the Pacific: National Case Studies* (Dordrecht: Springer, 2010).

Chapter One
The Rise and Consequences of Religious Diversity

Religious diversity has increased and along with it there has been a revitalisation of religion's role in public policy debates. These facts have caused many to be fearful that violent conflict will necessarily ensue; that societies like Australia, Canada and New Zealand will be fractured by religious rivalry and hatreds. The core challenge we face is to move from fear. But where to and how? We have been raised basically to fear diversity, it is in our cultural DNA as it were; diversity is seen as a problem to be overcome.

Some argue that for there to be peace we must all become one somehow, if only there could be just one religion—mine of course—we will be freed from this fear. We should all become one. We should all have the same faith, or for the atheists, we all should have none. If we did then we would have peace in the world. Of course that is nonsense. We are human beings. If we were all to get to look alike, somebody is going to say I am going to wear scarlet, just to be different. I am going to believe differently or I see it differently to you; my situation is different to yours, the way you see things does not apply to me. No religion is without its internal diversity of interpretation, regulation and application.

An Old Normal: Fear of Diversity

One of the main points of this book argues that calls for unity bring demands for uniformity and ultimately fail to be able to deliver the goods. We are not the same. Our religious diversities are real and not to be papered over or denied. I am an Anglican. I have my place and those of other denominations and religions can have theirs and we all can stand together and we do not have to fight, but we can and often do. Religious diversity, like any other difference can be the source of violence, but it does not have to be. The fear of religious diversity arises in part from our past experi-

1

ence with it and our expectations about it. The vision is to move beyond fear, to see tolerance as a helpful process on the way to understanding religious diversity's promise. Tolerance is a step along the way. We all hate tolerance. I do not like being tolerated any more than you do, but it beats being hit, denied, told I am not right, rejected and excluded. The challenge is to come to see religious diversity actually as part of that which is good, that which we should nurture. In time we may come to understand that cultural and religious diversity is as important for the sustainability of a society as biodiversity is for the sustainability of the biosphere.

Where do we get our fears, our drive for religious uniformity? The repression of religious diversity in the Spanish Inquisition and the European wars of religion in the sixteenth and seventeenth century were extremely violent, costing millions of lives, destroying much property and prosperity. They also gave religion and very bad name as each insisted it only was correct and all others had to be eliminated with the help of the state. Similar attempts to link religion with national identity with violent outcomes can be seen in the recent history of Sri Lanka, the rise of Hindu nationalism, and wars of ethnic purity in the Balkans. For those of shaped by Western culture the wars of religion provide a starting point. These wars ended in 1648 with the Peace of Westphalia which was designed to end all that violence that those who like to say religion is nasty, keep pointing to and we have to admit that religions were pretty awful at that point. Some argue that this was a major step in the emergence of the modern nation state. According to this peace wars of religion would end, because each nation was to have one prince, one religion, and one church. Interstate warfare could only be conducted for 'just purposes', which did not include differences in religion. The Prince would decide which religion was that of the realm producing a form of internal national social cohesion based on shared beliefs, values and the organisation designed to instill, apply and enforce them.

The framers of this peace and many social theorists after assumed that social cohesion and harmony required one state, one religion, one state church, a connection of mutual support between the two including such actions as tax support, or relief for the church, and support for the state in the form of bishops blessing cannons and ships, prayers opening parliaments, the use of the Bible in swearing in officers. It also assumed a relationship of mutual control. The state would control the church through appointments and the church would use the state to control its own internal diversity, for example by using the courts to try heretics. Such trials have been held in both Australia and New Zealand in the twentieth century. This problematic relationship between religion and the state continues to exist in our societies and is a much contested relationship here and in many other nations as the rise of religious diversity tests old ideas of how societies work.

According to this modern way of looking at societies, this 'old normal', diversity is not good. It had become normal to consider religious diversity as a symbol of weakness in the leadership of a society. Somehow the society had not got it all together; it has some bits that are only going to undermine the social cohesion, elements that are not firmly part of the social order. In this view of social life, which has been quite dominant until the last fifty years, only a very narrow range of difference was tolerated in all areas of life. Whether it was in marital life, sexual life, religious life, art life, educational life, there was no room for diversity. We all had to be same. When I was growing up those who did not fit in were said to be 'maladjusted' like some faulty radio or television set. There were those whose job it was to 'adjust' people and religion played a large role in this. We all had to line up pretty well together. From an institutional point of view, so long as you supported dominant values you might get away with a little bit of diversity, but you better be louder about your support for the core values and the established order, if you were going to be the least bit diverse. So long as you bolster the dominant group, you might be allowed a little bit of difference. Diversity was managed by the state, managed by the church, managed by education and it was   managed very tightly, in a controlling way.

The Passing of the Normal

The 'old normal' is gone. Religious and other diversities have undermined its basis in the populations of most countries. The passing of this old way of viewing things has been interesting to watch for anyone over sixty-five years of age. It is still echoing in the calls for cultural homogeneity and arguments against multicultural and multi-faith societies. Some argue that diversity is not new. Yes, there had been diversity in the past. Yes, you hear the stories of people moving around the former British Empire. There was a lot of movement of people, engagement with different cultures, ideas coming back from afar, but difference was still basically over there, or housed in museums.

What has happened since World War II has involved the kinds of migration and cultural changes that are producing a very different world? This process is often referred to as globalisation. Globalisation refers to the movement of capital, ideas and people around the world. Empire building moved people and ideas around, but post-war migration has brought cultural and religious diversity into the cities of the world in a way that was not there before. We feel it. When we go out in the streets, we see it. You do not have to go to Melbourne to find it, but, if you do, you will. You can find it in Wellington and Auckland. You can find it in small towns in Victoria. Farming communities which have welcomed migrants in order to keep schools open, maintain hospitals, attract doctors and other professional services, or to keep abattoirs open. In country towns like these, conservative rural people are heard to say 'welcome the refugees, the boat people, bring them to us, let them in, we need them for our economy'. If you were to go to a town like Seymour, or Cobram you will find a community of Muslims, some Buddhists, Hindus and others of recent migration whose presence and work keeps the local economy going and in the process finding new ways of living together in a richly diverse community.

In addition to religions moving around the globe through the migration of their adherents, globalisation has seen the movement of religious cultures and ideas sometimes through the work of missionaries, like the Church of Jesus Christ of Latter Day Saints—aka Mormons, through the Internet and books. We live in a constant wash of diversity as religious, political and other ideas boom around. Yes, they have boomed around for years, but there has been quite a flood of them as the number increases and as they are represented to us in the media, through members of our family and in our neighbourhoods.

People are constantly exposed to new religious ideas including 'Progressive Christianity', various evangelical forms of Christianity, Islam, Buddhism or certain kinds of Japanese religions that are easily available. Gurus abound telling us to do this, or do that and peace, or prosperity or both will abound. Spirituality is in. Go to a bookshop and there will be a spirituality section displaying rack after rack after rack of books about ways of being spiritual. And people pick them up, form a group, bring in a guru, find peace, and experience the mystical. Sometimes it lasts, sometimes it does not; but lasting is not the aim, enduring is not a postmodern virtue. It was what it was, on to the next. Pentecostal forms of Christianity are alive and well in Australia and New Zealand. They have the kids, the old mainstream Protestants have not, and the Catholics are losing them.

There is a rise of spirituality reflected in those people who say that they are spiritual but not religious. They reject organised forms of religion, but they pray, hold theological beliefs and meditate. Even those who say they have 'no religion' are very mixed about matters spiritual with some saying that they pray, meditate, and go to church.

I found it very interesting that, when there was an Atheist Convention in Melbourne, in 2009, some of the Atheists were behaving very badly by not only being very evangelical about their Atheism—which if they want to be, that is alright with most Australians and New Zealanders—but also by speaking very negatively about religion in general and people of faith in particular. While virtually no one objected to their right to be and to express their views, when they got to be disparaging about religions and people of faith, some people who had ticked 'no religion' in the census began to say, 'you know, that is not where I am. I do not want to be disparaging of what other people believe.' In some ways it seems that we are intolerant of intolerance and a bit leery of any one being to aggressive in the marketing of their views. Australians prefer matters of faith to be a more 'low temperature', not something to get overly excited about, or to either promote or oppose too vigorously.

The Emergence of Religious Diversity

Some Data

The emergence of religious diversity in Australia and the extent of it in both Australia and New Zealand can be seen in the census data available for these countries, which include a question about religious identity in the census they conduct every five years. Religious identity is simply the answer given in response to a question like, 'What is your religion?' The changes in the religious composition of Australia are given in Table One. Table One includes a rough prediction of where things will be in 2011. Given that recent surveys put the percentage identifying as Christian at less than 50% these predictions are conservatively optimistic.

Table One

Religious Change in Australia*

% in	1911	1947	1966	1991	2006	2021
Anglican	38.4	39.0	33.5	23.9	18.7	11
Catholic	22.4	20.7	26.2	27.4	25.8	21
MCPRU	26.5	22.1	19.4	12.9	8.7	5
CHRISTIAN	96.9	88.0	88.2	74.1	68.0	50
NONES	0.2	0.3	0.8	12.9	18.7	30
Other Rels	0.8	0.5	0.7	2.6	5.6	10

*Table excludes those who do not respond (11% in 2006)

Anglicans in 1911 comprised 38.4% of Australia's population. The high water mark for Anglicans in Australia was 1921, at 43%. Anglicans were never more than 50% and given current trends will be lucky to be 11% in 2021. Catholics have risen over that period largely due to migration to Australia from Catholic countries like Italy and the Philippines. Mainstream Protestants are labelled as MCPRU in Table One and include Methodists, Congregationalists, Presbyterians, Reformed and Uniting. If you add them up in 1911 they account for over a quarter of the population, but from that time on they steadily decline and they will be lucky to make 4% in 2021. The total claiming to be Christian in 2006 was 68% but given the rate of decline among major component groups they will be lucky to comprise 50% in 2021. The 'Nones'—those declaring no religion including atheists, rationalists and agnostics—have been steadily on the increase and are very likely to be about 30%, at least, in 2021. The continued growth of 'Other major religions'—especially Buddhism, Islam and Hinduism—the fastest growing world religion between 2001 and 2006--will probably bring these groups up to 8%. When the various smaller religions and spiritualties are added, the 'Other Religions' category will approach 10%.

Some cross national comparisons are in order to get a fuller picture of what is going on and to demonstrate that each country is different. Table Two presents data comparing Australia, New Zealand, Canada, The United Kingdom and the United States (Pew data).

Table Two

Cross-national comparisons of Religious Diversity

% IN 2001*/6**	AUS**	CAN*	NZ**	UK*	USA (2008)
Catholics	25.8	43.2	14.0	{}	23.9
Anglicans	18.5	6.9	16.9	{}	1.5
No religion	18.5	16.2	34.0	15.1	16.1
Not stated	10.0	{}	7.3	7.8	0.8
Uniting/ed	5.7	9.6	-	{}	6.2
Lutheran	1.3	2.0	0.2	{}	0.6
Presbyterian	3.0	1.4	12.4	{}	2.7
Orthodox	3.0	1.6	0.4	{}	0.6
LDS	0.3	{}	1.2	{}	1.7
Pentecostal	1.1	1.2	2.1	{}	5.9

Nations are very different as a result of simply their religious composition. Each takes its own composition as 'normal' and views others as deviant. This is particularly true of Americans. Part of the religious cultural cringe to be found in the antipodes is the propensity to try to adopt programs developed overseas without taking into account the very different contexts in which they were developed and at which they were aimed. Take the proportion claiming to be Anglican, for example. In Australia they have been very dominant and are now 18.5%, making them less numerous than Catholics, but in New Zealand they are much closer, while in the US there are hardly any at all, at 1.5%—but in the USA they make up for size with wealth. Meanwhile, in Canada Anglicans are fewer than United and those reporting 'no religion'. Catholics vary in proportion from 43.2% in Canada to 25.8% in Australia, 14% in New Zealand and 23% in the USA. New Zealand is outstanding in two dimensions by really leading the pack in those declaring to have 'no religion' in this census—32% is way ahead of the USA and Australia, if that means being ahead; and with 12.4% declaring themselves to be Presbyterians. New Zealand must be the only country in the world outside Scotland and North Ireland to have double digit Presbyterians.

Differences in the proportion of smaller Christian groups further demonstrate the importance of attending to cross-national differences in religious composition. I wish that data like these were available for the UK, but they ran a census with a religion question for the first time a decade ago. They made a botch of it, having failed to ask countries like Canada, Australia and New Zealand who have been doing a religious census for centuries for advice on how to do it. Australia has an excellent classification system for religious groups, but all the British wanted to know was how many Muslims they had. So all they had people do was tell you are you a Buddhist, Christian or Muslim or … They did not seek a clearer indication of which denomination of Christian they were. For a sociologist of religion that was cruel.

The nations we have been looking at also show variation in their proportions of other religious groups and traditions. Table Three presents data comparing five nations.

Table Three

More Cross-national Comparisons of Religious Diversity

% IN 2001*/6**	AUS**	CAN*	NZ**	UK*	USA (2008)
Christian	67.6	76.6	54.2	71.8	78.4
Muslim	1.7	2.0	1.0	2.8	0.6
Hindu	0.8	1.0	1.7	1.0	0.4
Buddhist	2.1	1.0	1.4	0.3	0.7
Jew	0.4	1.1	0.2	0.5	1.7
Sikh	0.1	0.9	0.2	0.3	
Baha'i	0.1		0.2	0.1	
Pagan	0.1	0.1	0.5	0.1	
None	18.7	16.2	32.3	15.1	16.1

The proportion Christian is the largest by a very large margin in each of these nations. There is no religious group in contention for that leading position among the other groups, even with the comparatively dramatic decline of Christianity over the last century. In both New Zealand and Australia Christianity is very likely to lose its majority position in the next decade. In New Zealand it is credible to anticipate the 'Nones' coming level with the Christians and overtaking them as the twenty-first century progresses.

The proportion from various world religions and other religious groups also varies across these nations. The USA has the smallest proportion of other world religions except Judaism in which case it leads. The proportions of Muslim vary but are about half of those found in Germany and France, which are about 4%. Hindus in Australia are growing rapidly due to migration from South Asia and are very likely to be over 1% in the 2011 census. The numbers and proportion of Hindus in New Zealand are also growing—257% since 1991—largely due to migration from Fiji. This brings to our attention another critical analysis in the analysis of religious diversity—the ethnic origins and compositions of the several religious communities. For example, Australian Catholics were predominantly Irish until the mid twentieth century when the migration of Dutch, Italian, and later Vietnamese and Philippine Catholics brought internal diversity to Australian Catholics.

A few more comments about the shape of religious diversity in Australia are in order. As of 2006 there were more Buddhists than there were Baptists, more Muslims than Lutherans, more Hindus than Jews, and four times as many Witches as Quakers. This last one is a really good sensitiser to the nature of an audience, because if I report this to a school group, or a group under forty years of age, they will ask, 'what is a Quaker'. They know what a Witch is because they watch it regularly on TV—for example Buffy the Vampire Slayer, or Bewitched. There is a lot of 'friendly' programming about witches on TV. But there is very little if anything about Quakers, and then it will not be on channels frequented by youth. And another tidbit of religious demography, we only have 31,000 people in all of Australia willing to say that they are atheists. Many report that they have 'No Religion,' but few claim to be atheists. Thus, it is an error to claim all of those who say, 'no religion' for the atheist camp.

Finally a comment on age and religion. Table Four presents data on the percentage over the age of fifty-five years of most religious groups in Australia. This is a lot of detail, but worth examining. A healthy religious group would have roughly the same age distribution as that of the whole country. Catholics come the closest and as the most numerous group we would expect this. However, many groups have a more elderly profile—Anglicans, Presbyterians, Reformed, Uniting, and Lutheran. These groups have well less than 20% 0–14 years old. More striking is their double-digit percentages in the 65–74 age group where the national picture has 7%. Presbyterians have a double-digit entry in the 75–84 group. Indeed 26% of Presbyterians are over 65. Jews at 22%, Anglicans at 20%, Uniting at 21% and Lutherans at 19% are not far behind.

Table Four
Age by Religion in Australia 2006

AGE Religious Identity	0-14 yrs	15-24 yrs	25-34 yrs	35-44 yrs	45-54 yrs	55-64 yrs	65-74 yrs	75-84 yrs	+85 yrs	Total
Christianity:										
Catholic	21%	14%	13%	15%	14%	11%	7%	5%	1%	5,126,880
Anglican	15%	10%	11%	14%	15%	15%	10%	7%	3%	3,718,252
Uniting Church	15%	11%	9%	13%	16%	15%	10%	8%	3%	1,135,427
Presbyterian & Reformed	9%	8%	9%	14%	18%	17%	12%	10%	4%	596,671
Eastern Orthodox (c)	18%	11%	14%	17%	12%	12%	10%	5%	1%	544,160
Baptist	19%	14%	12%	14%	15%	12%	7%	5%	2%	316,738
Lutheran	17%	12%	11%	14%	14%	12%	10%	7%	2%	251,107
Pentecostal	24%	17%	13%	15%	15%	9%	4%	2%	0%	219,689
Other Christian	21%	15%	13%	14%	14%	11%	6%	4%	1%	776,912
Total	18%	12%	12%	15%	14%	13%	9%	6%	2%	12,685,836
Buddhism	17%	16%	17%	18%	17%	9%	4%	2%	1%	418,756
Hinduism	19%	17%	25%	17%	12%	6%	3%	1%	0%	148,119
Islam	30%	19%	19%	15%	10%	5%	2%	1%	0%	340,392
Judaism	17%	12%	12%	12%	15%	14%	7%	8%	4%	88,831
Other Religions: Australian Aboriginal Traditional Religions	30%	19%	17%	15%	10%	5%	2%	1%	1%	5,377
Other Religious Groups	15%	18%	21%	18%	15%	8%	3%	2%	0%	103,645
Total	15%	18%	21%	18%	15%	8%	3%	1%	0%	109,022
Other religious affiliation (g)	15%	22%	24%	17%	12%	6%	2%	1%	0%	133,820
not stated	22%	14%	14%	14%	13%	10%	6%	4%	2%	2,223,957
No religion (f)	25%	17%	17%	15%	13%	8%	3%	2%	1%	3,706,555
Total	20%	14%	13%	15%	14%	11%	7%	5%	2%	19,855,288

More youthful distributions are to be found among Pentecostals (41% under twenty-five years of age), Muslims (49% under twenty-five years of age), Australian Aboriginal Traditional Religion (49% under twenty-five years of age) and 'no religion' (42% under twenty-five years of age) compared with a national standard of 34% under twenty-five years of age.

I just picked Adelaide to give an example of how rapidly some groups are aging. While Adelaide aged by 4.2 percentage points, The Uniting Church of Australia aged by 8.4 percentage points, Anglicans by 8.1, and Salvationists by 13.2

Table Five:
Age and Religion in Adelaide

% 55+ IN AGE	2006	1996
• UCA	43.1%	33.7%
• Anglican	41.6%	33.7%
• Baptist	33.0%	27.5%
• Lutherans	30.6%	26.2%
• Catholics	27.2%	22.6%
• Pentecostal	20.6%	14.8%
• Salvationists	44.0%	32.8%
• **ADELAIDE**	26.7%	22.9%

The Aging of British Protestants and Lutherans is further evidence of the passing of a particular form of Christendom. Census Canada reports that 'Some denominatons seem to have difficulty attracting younger members. The median age of members of the Anglican, Lutheran, Methodists, Presbyterian . . . and Uniting Church faith groups are in the range forty-three to forty-six years. This is significantly higher than thirty-seven years of age,

which is the median age for the Canadian population as a whole.'(http://
www12.statcan.gc.ca/english/census01/products/analytic/companion/
rel/contents.cfm). As a result of this aging it is becoming harder and
harder to find a breeding pair of Presbyterians, or Uniting, or Anglicans.
Given that the most sustainable form of church growth has been through
children born to existing members this avenue of growth or renewal is
no longer available. Those who are fifty-five years of age are still part of
the youth group. I am sixty-nine years or age and I have been part of the
youth group in my church for all my life. What is more telling is the fact
that those who attend are on average older than those who merely identify
making the average suburban church an increasingly geriatric assembly.
Such parishes had better have a hotline to the funeral director. From these
data it becomes patently clear that the form of Christianity that was dominant in the last century and the century before is literally dying out. The
outstanding religious change in New Zealand is the dramatic rise in the
number a proportion of the 'Nones'. This is the biggest change in religious
diversity, the huge rises in those saying no religion, 5 percentage points
in five years. Moreover, amongst those twenty to thirty-five years of age,
nearly 50% said they had 'no religion'. This does not mean they would say
no to spirituality, and it certainly does not say that they are atheists. They
are just saying that we are not showing up anywhere regularly to worship,
we are not associating ourselves with some formally organised religious
label. The question is, in terms of that movement towards no religion,
does New Zealand lead the way?

The critical difference that these changes in the religious profiles of
these nations have made is that most of our cities and most of our religious diversity is not segmented off into isolated communities. Changes
in religious demography have had personal and familial implications. The
religiously different are living next door. They are members of your family. They are shopping with you. They are in the streets alongside you.
We have not carved ourselves up into isolated religious communities geo-
graphically identifiably located. The exception is the UK, where Muslims
have populated the rust belt and seem to be trapped there after the jobs
left. But for the most part of the world, everyday life has become religiously diverse. And that is very different from the past; daily experience of life
and society is different. Associated with these changes is the sense that
societies are becoming both more religious and less religious at the same
time. How this is working out will be explored in the following chapters of

this book as we examine the ways these changes in religious composition play out as they through the society.

The Consequences of Increased Religious Diversity

In a very real sense those living in Canada, Australia and New Zealand have lost an old normal; a former worldview, a way of seeing things that is no longer tenable. A kind of Christendom has passed; it is not passing, it is gone. The old Anglican Empire religion, English protestant domination is passing. In French Canada the Catholic hegemony has passed. For example when you look at Anglicans in Australia they have been declining in Australia since 1921, Presbyterians started going down in 1910, Congregationalists started going down in 1901, Methodists started down in 1905 and continued on from there. In terms of the percentages of populations identifying with a Christian group the depression was a disaster. The economic corollary of these changes happened when Britain joined the common market and stopped importing meat from places like New Zealand and wheat from Australia along with other commodities and raw materials. What we are examining is the religious and cultural side to those changes. When I first came to Australia in 1979 there were still people around who called England 'home', even though they were five generations Australian. Comments like these used to send me giggling out in the corridor.

There is also a loss of the notion of the desirability or necessity of one state, one religion for social cohesion. We had the notion that we were a Christian society with a Christian nature with some Christian foundations. We now hear people trying to make the claim that we are a Christian nation on the basis of historical evidence. Maybe so, but there were other sources and other groups at work in nation building as well. Whatever, they cannot succeed in making that claim on the basis of contemporary demographic evidence. On the other hand, if you were to ask most any Muslim in Australia or New Zealand if these are Christian countries, and they will say that it feels very much so to them – the pattern of holidays, the assumptions, what is taken for granted is all very Christian. But while they may feel Christian to the non-Christian migrant, things are not Christian in the way that they were before. Not in the sense of being the taken for granted, normal assumptions about how the society operates. That is gone.

Diversity is the new normal. The rise of Pentecostal spirituality along with Muslim communities, Buddhists and Hindus has required making room, geographical, social and physical for mosques, temples, and other spiritual places. In Australia, the new Christian normal is Catholic. They are the ones that still have people under fifty years of age, schools, institutional resources and they are 27% of the population. Meanwhile most Protestant groups have really gone into decline. It appears from global studies that when religious groups lose their former power, numbers of adherents decline and once easy avenues of influence to government become more difficult—or at least shared, they become more strident and extreme in their demands. With the rise of religious diversity come questions about how to incorporate different languages, various cultures and diverse religions. How is a society, its schools, its social services and its work places to accommodate a wider variety of legitimate religious needs? I need this for my faith. I need Halal food. I need to wear this, or that. I need this day off. I need to be able to pray during the day. I need to do that. I need to bury my dead in this way. Are these going to be heard in respectful ways and accommodated? Or, will a once dominant group dictate to the minorities what they may or may not do?

For Australia dealing with these issues is relatively new as the society is gradually changing from being mono-cultural to being multi-cultural and multi-religious. For Canada, the change is from a bi-cultural society to one that is more inclusively multicultural, or to two coexisiting monocultural groups. In New Zealand it is different where the change involves going first from being mono-cultural to bi-cultural and now to, well, where New Zealand is going next is unsure as to how it will incorporate the several Pacific Island cultures and languages as well as the religious cultures of Muslims, Hindus and others. Even the role of Christian and other religious communities in the new environment is not clear. What is the place of the religious voice in the determination of policy and politics? Some are saying, get it right out of the public and civic domain. France says no religion in the public sphere, and they have been saying that since they took the heads off most of the bishops in the revolution. Turkey says the same thing, having acquired the secularist disease from France. However, that is not the only way.

The re-entry of religious voices into the public sphere.

Today more and more political philosophers are coming to grips with the fact that religious motivation for social action, religious understandings of policy issues and religious commitment has a place in the public sphere. But exactly what that role is and how to then negotiate when one religious or otherwise group's needs conflict with another group's legitimate needs. In 2010 I finished three years of research on freedom of religion belief in Australia. This area has proven much more contested than anticipated as various groups made clear their deeply held positions, concerns and desires. Out of the nationwide consultations has come a demand from some conservative Christian groups including Catholics and Sydney-side Anglicans that the full expression of their freedom of religion and belief includes the right of their social service agencies, schools and other church run organisations to discriminate in hiring policies on the basis of religious belief, gender, sexuality, marital status, and the capacity to reflect and represent the beliefs and values of the religious organisation. According to proponents of this view it is not only leadership and teaching positions that need to be limited only to those who subscribe to and live according to the beliefs of the religious organisation, the secretary and the gardener too may not be gay, or in a defacto relationship, or a single parent, or . . .

The contestation of religious voices with those based on other assumptions whether philosophical or political—there are no assumption free voices—raises such general questions as: What are the roles of these voices in the public domain? How are their conflicting demands to be moderated, or negotiated? How are community standards to be developed, discovered when there is no agreement about starting points? We do not have good mechanisms for doing these things because we have had an old accommodation between Protestantism and the basic assumptions about governance and social service provision. That old accommodation is gone and what is emerging is up for negotiation. The negotiation has been fully engaged by conservative and somewhat puritanical Protestant groups, who are often joined by conservative Catholics. Those who feel that the old accommodation will protect their interests, those who are not ready to enter the fray and engage the conversation will not be heard. If the Liberal Protestant compassionate voice is not going to become articulate, it will lose out to those who are less compassionate, but very articulate. This is not an easy time and the outcome is far from clear as those who think 'right thinking will prevail' because it is right will leave the field open to those who take narrow and less compassionate approaches to human rights and dignity. This debate presents a huge challenge for the century and we are just moving into it. How will Australia and New Zealand resolve the conflicting demands between those who would impose a restrained moral order and those who would implement a more laissez-faire one?

We have been discussing the rise of religious diversity and its consequences in the domain of public policy. Further consequences of increased religious diversity include increased interaction between and among religious groups and people who are religiously different. This has had the further consequence of religious revitalisation as religious voices re-enter the public domain and as religious identity becomes salient to human interaction. Increased inter-religious contact has become a daily occurrence for most people. It certainly is daily occurrence if you happen to be in social service provision or health provision. How are health and social service personnel to provide for not only linguistic differences, but for the differences of religious orientation in elder care facilities, hospitals, health care, income support, counseling, or whatever? Take the example of burial regulations. It took about twenty years for Victoria finally to change its laws so that Muslims could bury their dead in ways that accorded with their rights and requirements. Europe still refuses.

Familiarity with diversity

Increased religious diversity as a daily reality also produces familiarity with diversity. Suddenly people have friends, or family who are not of a similar religion and as a result of that familiarity, inter-faith and inter-religious relationships can be something that is part of the normal and become understood and not frightening. I have often heard a conversation that runs along these lines, 'I suppose X are Ok, because oh yeah, we've got Sam over here who happens to be an X, and she is, well I understand her and how her religion works for her, oh okay'. Thanks to religious diversity, we have the opportunity actually to learn about how religion works for different people, just by having them as friends or colleagues or listening, rather than just reading about a group in a book. While what Buddhists do in Thailand may be very interesting, it is possible to learn about Buddhism at home, what Buddhists do in Australia, or New Zealand because there are Buddhist communities in Wellington, Melbourne, Bendigo and many other places. The reality of religious diversity is no longer only 'over there'. It cannot be ignored.

Some people refer to this as the 'Aunt Sally' effect. Most of us have an Aunt Sally, someone who is quite different to the rest of the family in some way, this case she is religiously different. Sometimes she is actually the nicest person, but she is not strictly kosher, at least not according to the dominant views of the family, but yet she is so nice, you cannot just ignore it. Or she could be a complete pain in the neck. However, she serves to normalise diversity.

Here is part of my story. I grew up in Grand Rapids, Michigan, which is the diamond in the buckle of the Bible belt. I was raised in the Christian Reformed Church, a very conservative group of Dutch ethnic origin. They were very strict Calvinists. I read Calvin's *Institutes of the Christian Religion* when I was eleven years of age for self-defence in family arguments about theology. That was the only way my father's side of the family communicated, arguing about theology. Theology is wonderful stuff. I loved it, a great game. However, my mother's side never went to church. So I grew up very familiar with religious diversity. Moreover, they were the nice people from whom I learned about compassion, grace, forgiveness, and unconditional love. No, not from my father's side, no. Total depravity was the game on that side. My mother's side of the family were my 'Aunt Sally' breaking the normalcy or superiority of religious homogeneity and showing that goodness and grace have more than one source.

A further part of my own story that provides a foundation for my understanding of and involvement in religious diversity stems from the fact that I have been a religious professional in eight different denominations including running a Quaker church in upstate New York whilst doing my PhD at Cornell University. I know religious difference from the inside, and I do not reject any of those denominations I served. Each has its strengths and weaknesses. I was a Presbyterian for many years, did my theology at Princeton and served a church in New York City, the church of the Master Presbyterian in Harlem while the civic unrest was going on in the early 1960's. I was very much involved in community relations, working with people under stress. It was a wonderful time. Then I moved on to the Fifth Avenue Presbyterian Church where I learned about quality preaching, and it was a great experience as well. I served the United Church of Canada and then the Presbyterian Church of Canada before coming to Australia where I served the Presbyterian Church and since 1982 The Anglican Church.

I have always been involved in movements promoting social justice. My father was a sociologist and the family so identified with the movement for Black civil rights that the Ku Klux Klan burned a cross on our front yard in 1949. We also suffered during the McCarthy era. Friends refused to play with me as my father was accused of being a socialist—people confused being a sociologist and pro-civil rights with communism.

My involvement in inter-religious relations stems from early involvement in social justice movements joining with people motivated by different religious and other beliefs to work to alleviate poverty, tend to the marginalised and raise up the despised. These elements of my background form the basis, which drives me all along.

Increased salience of religious identity

We have seen that the consequences of religious diversity include, the loss of an 'old normal', increased participation of religious communities in public policy debates, increased interaction among people and groups from different religious backgrounds, and increased familiarity with religious diversity. Another consequence of increased religious diversity as a daily reality in the lives of most people has been an increase in the salience of religious identity. If we were all the same, religious identity would not distinguish us. It would simply be an uninteresting, boring feature. Now religious identity comes up in conversations and in planning social events. I have actually been asked what my religion was in Australia. This is frequently the case in the USA where religious diversity has been part of the landscape for a very long time, at least since the massive migration from 1890 to 1920. Gender is usually obvious, and age is apparent but it is necessary to ask about religion and ethnic background. It is increasingly necessary to know a person's religious identity just to be polite, to be a good host. Religious identity has become relevant for security reasons. Knowing a person's religious identity may help to understand how that person operates, why they are not available on Friday nights, why they do not drink alcohol, why ham salad sandwiches may not be the best lunch to offer and why salmon would be better, why they take quiet breaks at several times during the day, and the list goes on.

As religious identity becomes more salient so does being part of a religious community. What does it mean to work for social inclusion or exclusion? It is clear that social inclusion builds more harmonious and productive societies. Social policy debates about inclusion have a strong religious element. In the interests of social inclusion it is now necessary to have a very large platform when holding a civic meeting because of the kinds of religious leaders you have to include. One for Christianity might do, but probably more than one is needed, and after that you have to have quite a range of other religious groups represented. In some recent occasions representatives of those of no religion or atheists have been invited. Such public displays of diversity presents the reality of difference, it also legitimates it, it says you are here, you are real, you are part of this society, come on in. And the neat thing is, these groups are dead keen to be part of the society, to make their contribution; not just to take, but also to give.

I want to point to a particular example of a religious community that has become established in Australia since the 1970s and who have been doing more to promote healthy inter-religious relations than almost any other group by inviting people around to dinner. As a direct result of the efforts of this Turkish Muslim organization associated with the Gulen movement —The Australian Intercultural Society in Melbourne and Affinity in Sydney—literally thousands and thousands of Australians have sat down to dinner with Muslims over the course of the last ten years either in public settings or in homes. This has happened simply because this Muslim organisation has decided that this is one of the ways they are able to promote knowledge about Islam, social inclusion by building bridges that result in friendship and familiarity where there was ignorance, fear and suspicion.

The increased salience of religious identity raised the issue of providing education about religion. If you talk to small religious groups they will say look, we need education about religion in the schools because people do not know about us, who we are, where we fit and confuse us with other groups, or blame us for what may be happening overseas. People are ignorant, and acting out of ignorance and fear. Tell them what a Baha'i is, tell them what a Hindu is, tell them etcetera, etcetera. Knowing who your neighbour is helps build trust, respect and a productive harmonious society. Ignorance and fear do not.

This whole business of religious identity and being part of a religious community cuts a variety of ways. Religious community may be very helpful, nurturing, and supportive to migrants trying to make their way in the new society, very helpful. Religions have been profoundly helpful in that. On the other hand there are issues of community loyalty; this is my community, I have got to defend it, and another group may be doing hurtful things to my community over there somewhere. It does not make much difference which group you are talking about. Christian Evangelicals get very upset about what Muslims are doing to the Christians in parts of Africa, India and Indonesia. Or, you can turn it around and hear that Muslims who are very unhappy about what Christians and Christian societies are doing to them in Africa, and other places. The problem comes from treating local groups as though they are responsible for the actions of their compatriots overseas. There are also occasions when overseas conflicts get played out locally. The local impact of overseas events is not trivial. Which is why when people say, 'what about this group?', it is necessary to clarify whether they are talking about this group here, or this group there, or there, or there. In discussing religious groups it is terribly important not to tar a local group with the sins of that group elsewhere.

Religious communities like other communities feel part of a society when their symbols are part of the landscape. We have witnessed a great change in the horizons of Australian and New Zealand cities as once dominant spires of Christian churches are first of all drowned out by commercial buildings and then are joined by the domes, minarets and other architectural representations of faith. Some who feel threatened by the decline of their group and the rise of others begin campaigns to limit or eliminate the presence of the symbols of faith—minarets, head scarves, kips, and turbans among other things. One of my favourite Imams who is the senior Imam for New York City, when he heard that the Swiss were passing legislation to ban the building of any mosques with minarets, said, 'I do not care if they make us build it out of Swiss cheese, a minaret is not essential for a mosque'. By the way the Swiss have a total of about three mosques and none of them have minarets.

Much of what passes for islamophobia, whether it is opposition to the building of mosques, or opening Islamic schools, or to certain clothing is a reaction against the rise of diversity. It can be seen as a push to narrow what is tolerable, often involving a hang over from the 1648 mentality that saw diversity as dangerous and a source of weakness. However, Christianity is no longer the normal, but, on the other hand, neither is the secular normal in the way that it had become in the second half of the 20th Century. In the twentieth century, secular referred to a de-theistic form of Liberal Protestant background of tolerance, understanding and seeking social justice. During this time those who increasingly declared that they had 'no religion' had been born into one of the mainstream Protestant churches. However, today we are in a spiritual market place, a very vigorous spiritual market place where choosing prevails but choices are not permanent, and are often quite partial. People say, 'I'll have, this but not that'. In this context identities, including religious identities change, are much more fluid, flexible and are becoming even more fluid at this time.

Secular Societies

What does secular mean? We use the term, but there are many meanings. Yes, it means some form of separation of religion and state, but if you really want to have a fun, go compare the nations of the world as to how they do that. There are no two nations in the world that separate religion and the state or government in the same way and the differences among them are huge and significant. Yes, in secularity no one religious group is able to dominate the discourse. That is a very important place to begin, because where one group can dominate and feels that it is important to do so the more pressing problems in managing religious diversity begin to emerge. But secularity as we are beginning to experience it now means that religion and spirituality are out of control. They are out of control of the state; they are out of control of organised religion. There are no levers that either religious organisations or governments can apply to control them. The state cannot bundle it up and say you can only believe this and do those things. Some states try to control religion and spirituality by having a short list of approved groups, or by banning others, or by making it illegal to change one's religion or to convert others. Where nations try to do this, it requires draconian measures including the use of state violence and ultimately they invariably fail. Trying to draw a line between what is in and what is out is extremely difficult.

On the other hand, religions cannot control diversity within them. There is a great diversity within religious groups. Just try being a bishop; internal diversity will make your hair fall out. Cardinal George Pell gives the impression that he thinks he can control Catholics in Australia, and every time he does, they laugh. It can be really fun to watch. Being out of control both internally and externally is very important to understanding the roles of religion in society today. It does not mean that there are to be no religious voices in social policy, nor does this form of secularity mean religious free state schools.

Finally, a secular society does not have to be irreligious, anti-religious or non-spiritual. In this context it helps to distinguish between the secular and the secularist. The secularist would drive religion out of the public sphere and is generally anti-religion. Secularism is not a neutral standpoint, it is an ideologically committed world-view that would drive religion out, push it underground and limit it to the private sphere. Secularists are not objective, they are not independent, and they are not neutral, even though they like to claim to be. Secularism is another ideological perspective. Secularism is a part of the anti-religion part of the enlightenment project, which has become very Evangelical of late, very strident and fun to watch from that perspective. In contrast, the secular does not give priority to any religion or ideology but it acknowledges the role of all viewpoints in a healthy society.

So being faithful today means being a person of faith alongside others, making, sharing space for others, being a person of faith, a particular faith, enjoying it, being ready to talk about it, being articulate and listening, faithful in your own way, taking responsibility for yourself and negotiating creatively.

Some Further Reading

Bouma, Gary, *Australian Soul: Religion and Spirituality in the 21ˢᵗ Century* (Melbourne: Cambridge University Press, 2006).

Census Canada http://www12.statcan.gc.ca/english/census01/products/analytic/companion/rel/contents.cfm
Accessed 13 Dec 2010.

Nachowitz, Todd, 'New Zealand as a Multireligious Society: Recent Census Figures and Some Relevant Implications', in *Aotearoa Ethnic Network Journal* 2/2, August 2007 (no pages).

Taylor, Charles, *A Secular Age* (Cambridge MA: Belknap, 2007)

The Pew Forum, *US Religious Landscape Survey.* (Washington DC: Pew Forum on Religion and Pblic Life, 2008).

Thomas, Scott, *The Glogal Resurrgence of Religion and the Transformation of International Relations: The Struggle for the Soul of the Twenty-first Century* (New York: Palgrave, 2005).

Wuthnow, Robert, *America and the Challenges of Religious Diversity* (Princeton: Princeton University Press 2005).

Chapter Two
Responses to Diversity:
Road Rage on the Road to Heaven

'Road Rage on the Highway to Heaven; Sibling Rivalry Amongst the Children of the One God.' I think that is an apt title for a chapter dealing with a lot of the kinds of conflict that we are experiencing today. The papers are full of commentary about religious diversity, religious competition and religious conflict. However, distinguishing conflict and competition is one of the key things to learn in this chapter that deals with the role of 'negative othering' in producing and maintaining inter-religious conflict.

Religious diversity and conflict is not just something I study out there, but they have been a lived part of my existence from my birth and through all my life. And so I rehearse a little bit about myself. I have had a long-standing involvement in inter-religious relations starting from my birth. My father's family was never discovered outside a church, and my mother's family was never discovered inside. I learned theology from my father's family, and grace and compassion and love from my mother's side. Putting the two together has been a lot of fun in my life and that is an important part of who I am. I have been doing theology and sociology all my life. My father was also a sociologist, and he preached from time to time. So this involvement in things sociological and theological is a kind of Bouma activity for some generations back. I did have a great uncle—my grandfather's brother—who was tried for heresy. Unfortunately, unlike Sir Lloyd Geering in New Zealand, he was convicted, and the trial was so painful that he never fully recovered from that time forward in his life. He was a little soft on Karl Barth, and one was not wise to be soft on Barth in 1952 Grand Rapids, Michigan, where religious competition was intense and religious diversity was carefully monitored, with boundaries carefully policed and rigidly reinforced, each religious group set off against the other and claiming to have sole claim to truth.

I have myself been a religious professional in eight different denominations. I will not bore you with the full list, starting off in the Christian Reformed Church then becoming Presbyterian, running a Quaker Church for three years in up-state New York, being United in Canada and coming to Australia as a Presbyterian, and then becoming Anglican. I love them all. I have turned my back on none of it and take grace from each of them in their own way, but reside as comfortably as possible for the moment amongst the Anglicans.

I also know the marginality of migrant status, and in Australia, being a Yank is probably the most despised ethnic group of all the lot. I suspect that in New Zealand Kiwis are about as cruel to Yanks as the rest of the world, and of course we deserve it, but it hurts. I am familiar with inter-religious competition as I said and with religious conflict from my youth, so what I say is not just a matter of intellectual reflection on having read or studied or being out there; it comes from having been boiled in it from the time I was born. And so the study of and the promotion of healthy inter-religious relations is part of my life's work. My life's calling and religious vocation is to be involved as an activist and researcher in the management of religious diversity, very much involved in inter-religious activities.

Dealing with Difference

Diversity implies difference, and this chapter deals with what we do with difference once we detect it and decide to label it in some way as good, bad or indifferent. It examines how we work with difference. Once a difference is identified, especially if it is defined as an important difference in which some options are better than others, then the question becomes, 'What are the boundaries?' and 'Who is in and who is out?' With respect to any difference—gender, race, religion, politics, and so on—there has been a lot of contestation and change over time over boundaries, about who is in which category and which differences count. We have such contestation about difference, boundaries and what is acceptable difference at the moment. What happens at the boundaries is important. How does difference make a difference and what do we do with the difference that difference makes?

My basic argument is that globalisation has led to increases in religious diversity, which in turn have led to a kind of revitalisation of religion. And that, revitalisation itself, when coupled with diversity, can lead to increases in religious conflict and competition. Religious conflict will arise particularly, if groups engage in what I call 'negative othering'. When negative othering comes into inter-religious relations it provides the corrosive, nasty ingredient that leads to and enables some of the uglier things we see in the world today.

Religious Revitalisation

We have witnessed a great increase in religious diversity in most societies, but particularly in Australia, New Zealand and other nations of the Commonwealth. The first chapter of this book included a discussion about how migration which has brought sufficient numbers of Muslims, Buddhists, and Hindus and other groups, which along with conversion bringing Pentecostals and a host of spiritualities has resulted in the emergence of significant religious communities which are different to those present in Australia and New Zealand before. I noted that New Zealand has the highest percentage of those claiming to have 'no religion' amongst the Commonwealth nations and one of the very few nations still to have double digit Presbyterians, which is a thing to stand tall in whilst you can.

Increases in religious diversity have brought religion back into public discourse in a totally unanticipated way. Who, twenty years ago, would have thought we would be having these kinds of discussions today? Twenty years ago, it was so certain that religion was a thing of the past. Sociologist after sociologist rejoiced in the secularisation theory. I held out and said, 'Well colleagues, you know, it just is not probably going to go that way'. When I went to Cornell to do my PhD and said I wanted to study religion, my thesis adviser said, 'Why bother, Bouma? There is not going to be any religion by the end of the twentieth century'. I had the pleasure in 2005 of going to my thesis adviser and saying, 'Hey Don, have you looked out the windows lately?' and he said, 'Yeah, you were right Bouma'. We had a good relationship, but the religious revitalisation we now take as normal, nobody would have predicted in the 1970s.

Religious revitalisation is in part a product of the rise of diversity. Once you have diversity, you begin to have a whole change in the policy debate. Politics become different, you get values debates—does this or that group promote the right values? We will pick this issue up in the next chapter. People are searching for meaning, for the spiritual; but they are searching in a different way. People today are searching as informed consumers in a wide open market full of options, opportunities, and difference. People take charge of the ways they negotiate their spiritual and religious lives. As a result someone might do Zen Buddhist meditation on Tuesday, attend a Presbyterian lecture on Thursday, go to something else on Saturday, and the next week could bring an entirely different range of options for spiritual expression and exploration. Oh yes, those of us who have committed to something for life, to being something religious in a particular way may think that that such shopping around is scandalously shallow. You can excoriate such practices if you wish, but that is done at the cost of being out of touch with where people are today. Moreover, if you were honest with yourself, the answer to the question, 'Are you spiritual and religious in the same ways that you were twenty years ago?', would most likely be, 'No'. The point is people are searching, looking.

Fluidity is coming into the religion and spirituality market in a way that it was not there before. All you have to do is look at TV, look at the movies and you quickly notice everything from *The Da Vinci Code, Harry Potter* and *Angels and Demons* to *Avatar*. Time and time again, just look down through the list of the movies and notice that they have spiritual themes and wrestle with religious and moral issues. I love the *Star Wars* movies. People were complaining 'Oh, isn't that terrible?' because 75,000 Australians put down 'Jedi Knight' or some other term associated with *Star Wars* in their responses to the 2001 census. I said, 'Have you seen one of the movies? You get three sermons.' The injunction to 'Trust the force' and the blessing, 'May the Force be with you'. In these movies you get a well developed moral frame, a theological orientation, and a basis for hope all packed up in some whizz-bang kind of visual stuff. Pretty impressive, rather more engaging than the average sermon, to say nothing of Sunday School platitudes. Pursuing theological, moral and ecclesiastical issues in *The Da Vinci Code* and *Angels and Demons*, Dan Brown seems not to be able to write anything without making millions of dollars. If that is not enough, have a look at the *Harry Potter* phenomenon, the *Lord of the Rings* books, movies, videos and board games.

Then there are the Atheists. I love the atheists these days; they have beome so defensive. Have you not noticed? They seem to be on the back foot in the context of religious revitalisation. Some have begun behave like Evangelicals to get some more traction for their views in the community. Some of them are about as harsh as any hard line Evangelicals. They speak badly of others, they engage in negative othering. I find this interesting to watch and notice as a response to the religious revitalisation which is going against the grain of all their predictions. They are on the back foot, and have become much noisier.

But they are not the only ones that are noisier. As religious numbers decline, smaller religious groups, as they become even smaller, are heard to be nosier, more demanding. We get small pockets of Evangelical Christians trying to claim that New Zealand and Australia are Christian countries. I find that amusing. By what standards would such a claim be tested? They argue for certain policies as though they represent not just some majority or a significant constituency, but from some divinely given and historically unassailable position as the sole source of all that is good in society. On the basis of this some try to get particular legislation through which is usually aimed at denigrating or excluding this or that group, or narrowing the options of all to suit their views of what is best for society. Examples include opposition to Same Sex Marriage, abortion, euthanasia, or gambling.

Religious resurgence is happening everywhere around the world. I find it a very interesting thing to watch. As the republics of the former Soviet Union lift the repression off religion, you get huge growth. The end of the Cold War has brought new forms of ideological conflict involving religion. Religious revitalisation has taken the form of some increased participation in religious activities in some places. However, it is just not happening amongst the old mainstream, I regret to report. Yes, the old British Protestant mainstream will be there forever, I am sure, but not in the powerful way that it was in 1950. The current religious resurgence will not restore British Protestant Christendom. It will not bring the churches back to that level of power, prominence and prestige.

Why Revitalisation?

Some people ask 'Why is religious revitalisation happening?' Surely the long term is going to be decline. And I remind them, look at history and you will note the ebb and flow of different forms of religious involvement, various forms of religious organisations, and different styles of spirituality. Those who take the 1950s to 1960s to be the normal, to be the standard by which other times are to be judged, take a highly specific period of religious life. Why pick it? The fact that it was the reality of the youth of today's older generation is not an adequate explanation. A look at history can be so revealing and provide understanding of the ebb and flow of religious life. History reveals that the foundations of Australia and New Zealand are quite different. Australia was founded at a time when the religious life of Britain was at its lowest level for a long time. One of my favourite statistics, and there will not be many more of these, is that the Eucharist attendance at St Paul's Cathedral in London on Easter Sunday in 1800 was six. Most convicts did not have regular church involvement as part of their pre-transportation lives. The presence of the churches was not really felt in Australia until the 1830s and 1840s when the state partnered with churches to civilise, educate and care for people. In contrast, New Zealand was founded when things religious were up and coming in the United Kingdom, when the whole business of building churches through Britain and especially in the burgeoning urban areas. The expansion of the non-conformists, the expansion of the Church of England, was supported by governments as part of a new compact between society and church. That compact, that association has peaked in about 1960, it has been waning and much is changing. These changes make some feel afraid, others seek to restore the past, and still others try to re-invent it. Whatever is happening, religion and religion and society issues are not just simply going to go away as was predicted in the 1960s, '70s and '80s.

One of the more powerful drivers of religious revitalisation has been the failure of secular humanism to deliver on its promises. The whole promise that with the adoption and legislation of secular humanist policies and ideologies a kind of nirvana was going to dawn upon us and was going to produce happiness and health and welfare for all, keeps running smack against the hard surfaces, and cold brick walls of failure. The fact that this approach is not getting anywhere, is not providing the sought after panacea, begins to force people back to basic questions about what is going on? What do I believe? What do I need? Who and what can I trust? What can take me through the difficult times? Secular humanism did not end oppression, end poverty, or cure pain, and it did not provide much motivation to end social justice. Again a review of the history of the great movements of social justice reveals that each of them had its roots in religion, leaders motivated by religious compassion and at least in the West, usually in Christianity. If you cut off those religious roots, motivation wanes and social justice movements wither failing to have the energy to survive the long hard work. Secular humanism failed to deliver on its promises. These failures begin to feed into a rise in religious revitalisation as some choose to explore religious avenues of understanding, meaning and community.

Religious Diversity and Religious Rivalry

When religious revitalisation is coupled with an awareness of religious difference, issues of inter-religious relations emerge that had not been there before, at least not to the same degree or intensity, or which had been sort of kept down, repressed. We spent the twentieth century trying to be nice to each other in Christian ecumenism. Increased religious diversity has produced another form of revitalization—increases in the salience of religious identity. When the great majority of Australians were Anglicans or British Protestants, religious identity made little difference. It simply was not interesting. The religious divide that did count was Protestant vs Catholic sectarian conflict. However, if we are all the same, who cares? We will find something else to differentiate ourselves on: the footy team we barrack for, North/South Island differences in New Zealand, Quebec / Rest of Canada, the on-going Melbourne/Sydney rivalry or whatever other form of difference there is around, but not religion. However, when we are different religiously, then suddenly that difference becomes a potentially interesting part of our identity, something that is useful in describing your self to others, something others 'need to know' about you to understand you.

In the twentieth century we even largely overcame the Protestant vs Catholic divide. The impact of Vatican II in this regard was enormous as Catholics were given theological and institutional frameworks promoting mutual respect and interaction. The fact that in both Australia and New Zealand Catholics now out-number Anglicans and British Protestants helped this. However, ecumenism often proceeded by denying difference, differences which for the most part were and remain patently obvious. Such denials of difference are painful to those who value them. The denial of difference says to them, 'What is important to you, just does not count. After all, we are all the same really.' Where I grew up, if anybody said something like that, they got laughed out of the place. Among Dutch Calvinists there was a foundational principle for ecclesiastical organisation, which was summed up in the aphorism, 'you cannot split dead wood'. A quick look at their history will reveal that Presbyterians had a pretty good way of following similar lights in insisting that theological and liturgical differences counted. So we always found something to be different about.

I find it interesting that in the twenty-first century The Catholic Church has begun to re-assert its distinctiveness and to put up barriers to easy movement across denominational lines. This was painfully and forcefully brought home to me when I was explicitly informed that I, as an Anglican and non-Catholic, would not be welcome to receive the sacrament at the requiem mass held for a close friend and colleague. This was a radical reversal from the pattern I experienced in the 1980s and 1990s. The shift to increased attention to boundaries and barriers is seen in the change in the welcome extended to non-Catholics in Paris and West France. I served an Anglican Chaplaincy in Dinard in Brittany for a number of years. In 1992, the Anglican parish of St Bartholomew's held the Christmas Eve Carol Service and many Catholics attended filling the church to over 200 souls. We then adjourned to ND de Dinard for the first Mass of Christmas Eve at which my Anglican parishioners were welcome to receive the sacrament AND I con-celebrated the festal mass with the Catholic Curé. This would not happen now. The point of this is not to criticise Catholics, although I miss the camaraderie, but to note how with the rise of the importance of religious difference, boundaries are being marked and patrolled.

Competition vs conflict

The rise of boundary maintenance raises the issue of inter-religious relations in conditions of diversity, particularly where no one group commands a majority, or can claim to be the dominant group demographically or even culturally. Are religious groups to engage in competition or conflict? It is very important to distinguish the difference between competition and conflict. Once you have religious difference and you pay attention to it, it is a quick step to either competition or conflict. Seldom do people say, 'Oh, we are different, so what?' Rather difference is quickly followed by competing or conflicting. What is the difference? In competition, competitors respect each other. This is one of the foundational differences between competition and conflict. In competition, parties act within some kind of sets of limits, if not agreed, they might be imposed. Competition is regulated, respectful, and full on but one major difference is that competition does not involving 'negative othering' like occurs in conflict.

However, in conflict, one party seeks to drive the other out, to eliminate the competition, to annihilate the other. One group seeks to deny the right of the other to exist. For example, Evangelical Christian groups might oppose the building of mosques because they do not want Muslims in their town, or because they consider Islam a threat to their society, or demean it as 'a false religion', or seek to defend the Christian nature or feel of their society. Similarly, such groups might oppose Muslim schools order to keep Islam out, and to keep Muslims from successfully raising their young in the faith. Some go so far as to argue that certain religious groups are not to be admitted as migrants to their country. These are examples of inter-religious group conflict as in each example one group seeks to eliminate the religious other, to deny their existence, their right to be.

Negative othering

In the process of inter-religious conflict, one group often dehumanises the other. In so doing the language of 'negative othering' is used, saying, 'You are less than fully human in some way'. Persons of religion X, or belief Y, or practice Z are declared to be lesser in the eyes of God, less than fully human. Religion X is a false religion, or a religion of Satan. People are told that by doing X, or believing Y, you have chosen to do or believe certain things that make you 'less than human'. This is the rhetoric of negative othering. Such rhetoric will be familiar from the rantings of the Reverend Ian Paisley in the context of Protestant vs Catholic conflict in Northern Ireland. It is also heard in Hindu vs Muslim conflict in South Asia, and in the anti-Muslim speech that has escalated in some Western countries particularly since the events of September 11, 2001.

What is well known and is evidenced in the examples just given is that the rhetoric of negative othering leads some to commit violence. It is a rhetoric that legitimates violence and it produces violence. An example of religiously motivated violence occasioned by the use of negative othering rhetoric is found in the instances of those Evangelical Christians in the United States of America who from time to time blow up abortion clinics, or shoot health care professionals associated with them. Attacks on mosques, Sikh gurduwaras, Hindu temples, and Jewish cemeteries are associated with rhetorics of negative othering and increase following the outbursts of those who claim the right of free speech to vilify their neighbours. But examples also include those Muslims who take a negative view of the West, demean those in the West with rhetoric of negative othering and provide religious legitmations for terrorist activities.

Violence toward others requires negative othering rhetoric to motivate such actions. Violence requires that kind of de-humanising talk about the other. Seeing the other as less than human helps to permit treating them inhumanely. Such rhetoric was, and is, essential to all forms of slavery, to repression, and to physical violence. Most of us have lived long enough to have been through the odd war, and should be familiar with how quickly we get into negative othering in war time when we have an enemy as opposed to a competitor. So too, if you talk about another religious group in that negative othering kind of way, the de-humanising and the denial of the very right to be there begins to set up the ability to do the very nasty things to them that you would not do to someone you respected.

This is where the notion of 'road rage' used in the title of this chapter comes in. If we are on the highway of life together and conflict with others over a parking place, lanes of the highway, or right of way, we often start using negative othering about the drivers in other cars. That alone is bad enough, but as we know from all too regular news reports such negative othering in some occasions does proceed to aggressive driving including attempts to barge the other off the road, or worse to a violent attack. The rhetoric of negative othering has consequences. If you listen to the argumentation put by those who take an exclusivist view to their own presence in this world, such as exclusivist religious groups, the slide into using negative othering comes very early, very quickly and it is very hard to stop it from cascading into motivating negative actions toward the other, including violence. While not every person reacts to the rhetoric of negative othering by perpetrating violence toward the other, there are those in any group who are prone to violence, or who feel it there duty because they are able to do something and who indeed will act it out fully.

An example may help to clarify to distinguish competition from conflict. Groups in competition may use the state to further their aims. A group might, as they do in Australia, appeal to the state to support their faith based schools, or to support a program of social justice, or to put into practice some of the values that are important to the group. Such appeals would be put forward in the context of other voices, religious and otherwise, expressing competing views about the shape and order the society. This is what is going on within our legislatures all the time. It is very interesting to watch that process and observe the arguments made. However, this process can become problematic.

There is a certain logic among religious groups that argues 'If we can, we must'. 'If we can legislate a law that limits a behaviour we consider immortal, or protects an arrangement we consider important, or advantageous to our group and can think of religious reasons to do so, we must do it.' Watching competition degenerate into conflict often happens when a groups finds itself holding electoral majority. For example in Grand Rapids, Michigan in about 1954, we Dutch Reformed found ourselves in a position of an electoral majority, and we knew that we could put in a civic ordinance that came right out of our deeply-held values that would of course make Grand Rapids a better place for everyone, not just us. We banned bingo. Why? The theological argument was an anti-gambling ethical stance. The political strategy was pure conflict. Banning Bingo was seen as a very effective anti-Catholic strategy. Bingo was banned because that was where Catholics got their financial support. Doing this moved beyond competition and into the zone of conflict, attacking the right or ability of the other to survive.

History provides plenty of examples of where a group finds itself having some kind of legislative capacity to impose a particular rule and does so. That is just as true for the secularists. They too have values and concepts of the ideal society, which they too want to put into practice, to make real using the law of the land to do so. That is why a lot of religious groups feel put upon these days, saying, 'Look, those secularists have power and they are pushing us around. We want to push back.' Accommodating conflicting or competing ideas of the good society is a very, very difficult job for a society today, because we do not have a single shared value base, or belief system to appeal to enable us to have a shared foundation for making a judgment about these things. This is the challenge of religious and cultural diversity, which becomes evident time and time again as groups compete to shape the society according to their views. For Calvinists this meant to act according to Calvin's 'third use of the law'. For Calvin, following Augustine, and similar to Aquinas, the 'first' use of the law is to convict the sinner of sin and the second use is to provide the sinner with a model for living. But, the 'third use of the law' is to use the law to shape the society to make it a better place than it would have been had you not done so; shaping it according to your views of what is right and wrong; your understanding of the laws of God given in Scripture. In the state of Iowa, where Calvinists had an electoral majority they closed the cinemas. The Christian Reformed Church had decided in 1922 that cinema attendance was one of three forms of 'worldliness' and 'worldliness' was forbidden. Dancing and card playing were the other two.

When I was growing up there was a very long list of things we were not permitted to do on Sunday—sport, swimming, concerts, work, homework, all were forbidden. The list that you could do was a whole lot shorter. The State of Victoria, in Australia, like many other places in the Commonwealth used to have Sabbath legislation that forced everyone to 'keep the Sabbath' even if they did not share the religious beliefs of those who considered this so important that they legislated compliance for all. So no

Australian Rules football on a Sunday—and certainly not on Good Friday, no commercial trading, no . . . This made Christian church attendance about the only thing that was available. While this has now past there are still those who would use the state to enforce their views in various areas of life and there are those who are very watchful to ensure that such laws are not enacted that enable the minority to push others around.

Competitive Piety

The problem of enforcing rules, mores, and regulations is also felt within religious groups. It does not take much to raise the whole problem of internal rivalry. Issues of conflict vs. competition business arising from diversity are not just out there; they are also very present inside religious groups. When internal rivalry within religious groups about norms, values, and beliefs arise, you get what I call competitive piety. Competitive piety is one of the ugliest forms of religious life that I know of. The logic of competitive piety takes the following form: If I give up X but you give up X plus Y, you must be closer to God; If I am willing to sacrifice 10% of my income and give it to religion, but you are prepared to give up sex, or sacrifice your life, then you must be closer to God, preferred by God, more loved by God. This kind of logic leads to many forms of extreme self-sacrifice engaged in to compete with others in a form of sibling rivalry for the love God.

The logic of competitive piety leads to some very strange things happening. We are prone to see the silliness, ugliness, or tragedy of competitive piety in others, failing to recognise it when it happens in our own group. For example, there was a controversy recently when some Muslim cab drivers refused to accept passengers who were carrying bags of duty free alcohol out of the airport; or not being willing to take passengers who had dogs, including seeing-eye dogs. The community was outraged; they argued that cabbies were providing a public service. Were they not required to accept all and any passengers, by law? Perhaps the cabbies' rejection was understandable if the passenger was so drunk the alcohol was tipping out of them, but if it is just carried in a bag, where will this end? Next, someone will object to taking me, because my lunch contains a ham sandwich. The issue has gone quiet, but is not settled.

Competitive piety may be less harmful if a person simply organises their own life according to strict principles. But it seldom stays with the person. It affects others as they may be drawn to a more strict or harsh version of the faith and practice because of the examples of either the extreme few, or those who Max Weber would call religious virtuosi. Where I draw my moral line or my belief line, may be up to me, but often begins to affect others. I believe something even sillier than you believe; I must be closer to God. Unfortunately we seldom hear of competitive piety working in this way; I believe in doing something even more compassionate, forgiving and wonderful; I must be closer to God. However, competitive piety and sibling rivalry for the love of God often produces internal rivalry and conflict within religious groups. It often divides churches, synagogues and other religious communities and makes for the very, very bad press for religious groups.

Competitive piety leads to fierce internal dissension, Evangelicals versus Liberals versus Pentecostals; Shiite versus Sunni; Jewish groups taking very different views on the demands of the law. Competitive piety is often associated with movements to purify, to re-establish a group. Puritanical movements are very strong within Judaism, Christianity, and Islam. Such movements are strong within various forms of the other religions of the world, as leaders vie with each other to try to come up with a pure form, the right way, the one only way. Those who find puritanical movements most appealing are often those who know least about their faith, or about religions. Extreme forms of religion appeal to some children who were raised by secular parents. People who have been to a madrassah, or people who have been to a religious school, people who have been theologically educated know about the diversity and nuances within their theological and religious history. But if you do not know of this internal diversity, about the debates and conflicts of the past, you might fall for the A4 version of Islam or Christianity, whatever else, which says, 'Believe this and this, do that and that, and hate those'. It is very interesting to see who is susceptible to competitive piety and puritanical styles of religion.

When competitive piety becomes linked with negative othering it can become very dangerous as competing levels of hatred become expressed in violence. There has been increased religious conflict in recent decades. In the Cold War, the West, the Christian West had a common enemy—atheistic communism. Having a clear and non-resident enemy over there made things so simple, so black and white. The Cold War had a deeply religious element to it as the West, and particularly the USA, lined up its weaponry and personnel against Russia and China. With the passing of the Cold War it has been easy for some slip over into turning Islam into the new form of godless communism, except now it is the secular

West against altogether too-godly Islam, or for some Christians a battle between Christianity and Islam. Negative othering comes easily when times are complex and people become fearful. Negative othering clarifies the pictures, locates blame and sets up conflict. A person not prepared to engage in negative othering becomes suspect. 'Which side are you on? Oh, you are soft on Muslims are you? Oh well, I don't know. Well, Make up your mind. They cannot both be true . . . ' and on it goes.

Diversity and Boundary Marking

Who is in, who is out? Us versus them. Boundaries are coming back into the picture. In conflict, the other is denied the right to exist, as in the cases of opposition to building mosques, temples, schools, and denying particular groups the right to come in through immigration. Boundary marking between groups, including religious groups, can also involve demonisation, vilification, and dehumanisation of the other. Dehumanisation is critical to the process of negative othering. When you have dehumanised the other, you can then do all sorts of things to them you would never consider doing to a fully human other.

Boundary definitions between groups are changing in what might be called high modernity, or post-modernity. The distinctions of the recent past even as recently as the 1960s involved differences amongst groups which were organisationally distinct, hierarchically organised in denominations with head offices which were very much linked with the state. I am sure the former New Zealand Prime Minister, Robert Muldoon, but often referred to as Piggy Muldoon, talked to the Anglican Archbishop regularly and probably also to the Moderator of the General Assembly of The Presbyterian Church in New Zealand. A careful conversation between the three of them would have sorted a lot of issues out before they were ever considered as legislation. Religion was held in and controlled by organisational containers that provided people with identities, services and meaning. Yes, there was some movement between them, but not a whole lot. It was all very organised, very hierarchically controlled. Different groups had their inter-group connections at top levels. National coordinative councils had clear lines of authority, were marked by clerical domination; the clergy ruled. It was all very professionalised, very bureaucratic. Religious organisation was very much characterised along the same lines as the way the society was organised up until about forty years ago. Many people over fifty-five years of age would be very much familiar with that.

However, now things are different. Religion is out of control. It is out of control of both religious organisations and it cannot be controlled by the state. The boundaries between groups are less legal. Relationships, institutions and organisations are more fluid. People are more likely to wander around. Not everybody who comes, for sake or argument say St Andrew's on the Terrace in Wellington, was born and raised a Presbyterian, although it is a Presbyterian Church. People are more likely to be shopping; looking for something, and will only continue to attend somewhere because they like it. The boundaries are less enforced. They are also less enforceable by the state, by social opinion, or by anything else.

Now at the very time that the boundaries between religious groups are becoming more fluid, people are attending to them more. That is one of the interesting apparent contradictions of the moment; boundaries are being attended to more at the very time they are becoming more fluid. On the other hand, if there was no movement, no fluidity, they might be less interesting. However, just as boundaries are becoming less fixed and as a result harder to detect, there will also be more anxiety about them. How do I know if I am in or out? How do we know if someone is with us or against us? Along with that anxiety comes a focus on trying to find boundary markers, flags or symbols that tell whether you are one of them or one of us, little ways of detecting or expressing identity and association. There will also be more conflict as people move around and encounter boundaries in situations that they had not expected.

With increased anxiety about boundaries due to their fluidity, there will be more tightening of boundaries and there will be more negative othering. Why? Because when a person or organisation engages in negative othering, they declare a boundary and say, 'That is on the other side. You are not us!' So at this time, I find it very interesting that as our boundaries have become more fluid, as religion has become more interesting, then who is in and who is out has become once again interesting. The very fluidity of boundaries is associated with greater anxiety and people spending more time worrying about where the boundaries are. And with that comes an increase in road rage.

What are we doing when we engage in road rage? Why engage in negative othering? Road rage is part of the process of defining boundaries. I find interesting to hark back to my youth again; we knew the difference between those who were part of the Christian Reformed Church and the Reformed Church in America. Now, a person from Mars, or even Ohio, would have no hope at telling the difference ethnically, culturally or theologically, but they the RCA were 'oncers'. They only went to church once on Sunday; we CRC always went twice, hence of course we were closer to God, but the boundary was very simple. They were also a little bit light on the necessity of Christian education. They did not require their children to go to the denominational schools, and of course they went into more speedy decline than we did, which only ratified our sense of being closer to God, or better loved by God.

But then there was also a difference between us and the Baptists. This difference was very simple to tell, and you would find it out very quickly if you were in a mixed group and started talking about what you were going to do on a Friday night. We could not go to movies, we could not dance, and we could not play cards. The Synod of the Christian Reformed Church had declared those three activities to be forms of worldliness in 1922. But Baptists did not use cosmetics, they could not drink and were forbidden to smoke. These religious purity stands became markers of inter-group identity and boundaries. Viewed from 2010 these seem slightly funny, but they actually began to divide people off, because if you planned to go out and have a drink; they could not come. If they planned to play cards, or dance; we could not go. They could go to a movie; but we could not do that. Inter-group divisions marked by little flags.

It has been interesting to me to note that since 1995, there has been a growing publication industry amongst Evangelical Protestants in the United States and moving from there out into the rest of the world which is producing literature which vilifies Islam. 'Not the same God' type literature. It is a fascinating industry, which has produced now hundreds and hundreds of books, seminars, articles, and television programs. Taking an anti-Islam position has become an absolute test of whether you're really an Evangelical or not. It is one of two essential markers. The second is taking an anti-homosexuality position. That huge publication production has since 1995 and when it was last studied in about 2005, has had a considerable effect on the orientation of Presidencies in the United States, of Christian denominations, and has the capacity to undermine the work of those who seek to promote interfaith understanding and respect. The literature amounts to a massive demonisation of Islam; a demonisation of Muslims that forms the litmus test for acceptance as an Evangelical Christian. Does this literature sharpen the understanding of the cores of the other religious group? No, it is not written to illuminate but to instill fear.

Boundaries come up again in discussions of which groups are acceptable. In the context of increased competition among religious groups now, some groups are being more concerned about maintaining their ethos, maintaining their distinctiveness, and protecting what it is that is core for them. In an attempt to protect their core, some groups attend more to the boundaries than they do to the core. This becomes evident in the debate about allowing religious groups exemptions from civil rights legislation. Religious groups have appealed for exemptions from human rights legislations so that they could discriminate in their hiring practices against people whose presence in their schools and in their social service agencies would be deemed to violate their core values. That a Catholic school would find the presence of a raving atheist to undermine core values is understandable. However how is it that all gays, any de-facto couple, every single mother, and all pagans threaten core values? I have already discussed the boundary marking use of an anti-homosexual stance. However, Catholics and the Orthodox have major concerns about pagans. When I mention that many Australian Aboriginals could be classified as Pagans, they try to wiggle out, by saying that is not what they mean. This makes it clear that their negative othering of pagans relates to an image of the other, not to the actual other. I have not met a Catholic yet who tries to uphold this position that has met a real pagan.

Real vs Imagine Others

The opposition to pagans, and for that matter, opposition to people in same-sex and de facto relationships demonstrates the role of imagination in the process of boundary construction and negative othering. The role of the imagined other in this entire process is utterly critical. It is our imagination of the other that we fear, that we condemn, that we dehumanise. It is our imagination of what the other is like that we dislike. It is our imagination of the other shaped by negative othering that enables us to dehumanise the actual other. We create imagined communities of otherness, them. We create images of them, imagine fictions about them, and then begin to believe our imaginations, and fear the images we create. Dehumanisation is directed against an imagined 'them'; somebody not actually present to us; somebody whose fullness of reality we either do not admit to experiencing; or have not had occasion to experience. The imagined other is not encountered as a real person or as a real group with whom we have been able to talk, share, or come to understand.

We have anti-vilification laws in the state of Victoria. I supported their coming in. I was part of the case that was brought against the Catch the

Fire Ministries group who continue to run seminars on Islam. I was an expert witness on the role of vilification and the role of Islam in society. There were two Anglican priests involved in this. There was another one on the other side, who was very much promoting the right of a particular religious group to describe Islam in very negative terms with the result of making some Australian Christians fearful of their Australian Muslim neighbours. One argument put forward by those who oppose Anti-vilification legislation is that it prevents robust debate. An examination of the legislation makes it clear that it certainly does not prevent debate. But what was going on in these seminars was not robust debate. It would seem to me that if you are going to have a robust debate, you have a real Muslim and you have a real Pentecostal and they really need talk to each other. Robust debate does not occur when side simply excoriates the other. If the other side is not there, it is not a robust debate. I would have thought that dehumanisation and vilification would be prohibited by the commandment against bearing false witness about your neighbour because most of it is false, so framed as to produce fear and distrust and dehumanisation.

The outcomes of negative othering

Negative othering, including vilification and dehumanisation seldom stays at the level of rhetoric. Our fearful reactions to our negative pictures of the imagined other often express themselves in negative actions. The problem comes when this imagination goes the obvious next step and produces the real othering, produces discrimination, or violence. I have got scars from my youth during the McCarthy era in the USA, which was a time of 'commie' bashing. My father was a sociologist, he was in favour of civil rights, and he was in favour of public housing, all of which were pretty scandalous in the Kent County Republican stronghold I grew up in. He was accused by some as being a 'Pinko', soft on socialism and communism. I worked with him in this, and so I was told I was not welcome on sports teams, or to attend parties. I too was declared by some to be a Pinko. Indeed we were so well known to be in support of the civil rights movement that the Ku Klux Klan burned a cross in our front yard. Negative othering can have violent outcomes.

The negative othering of gays is the other litmus test for being an Evangelical today. You have to hate gays and you have to hate Muslims. If you do that, you are right as rain. However, this negative othering can result in denying accommodation or employment to gays. The negative othering of gay people, like all negative othering has consequences. For, example, if you happen to be in a social service agency run by a particular church, and a gay person comes to you needing accommodation and you will not provide the service; or you fire a single mother from your school, negative othering begins to have consequences for the lives of other citizens of the society. Just as denying Muslims the right to build mosques, or organising protests around the building of Muslim schools has consequences for the ability of these groups to prepare their children to take their places in the society. Remember, nearly 40% of Australian Muslims have been born in Australia. This is their home. It does not feel good to be excluded from home.

Negative othering is not without consequence. It can be seen to lead to violence against the other, violence against Muslims, violence by Muslims against Christians, violence against Sikhs, Buddhist violence against Hindu and Christian Tamils in Sri Lanka, violence against Asians, the West, abortionists, and the list goes on. Negative language is not without consequence and that is why I promote anti-vilification legislation and careful scrutiny about what is said about the other, for our language is not without consequence.

Road Rage

So why do I use the term 'road rage'? I think it actually fits what is going on around us in this time of religious inter-group conflict and competition, but particularly in conflictual situations. Most road rage takes place within the car, involving only the driver, or at most the passengers. I may rage and people who drive with me know that I am occasionally verbal as I drive along about some imagined other in another car, someone I accuse of being clearly incompetent (dehumanising), who probably has no business being on the road (denial of right to exist), clearly ought to be taken off the road. But this all happens within the car. It is very important to realise that most of our negative othering takes place within, behind closed doors. It does not have immediate consequences outside the car. The target of the negative othering is not an actual person but it is directed against the image of the other, my fiction of the other. It does not involve a real other.

The imagined other is the target of this negative othering, not the real person. But negative othering gets totally out of hand when the driver gets out of the car, particularly if the other driver also gets out of the car.

Matters quickly escalate from name-calling and exchanged accusations of incompetence or worse. Violence is well known to ensue in some cases. We know how negative othering proceeds on the road, when it takes the form of road rage. In the event that someone is already fearful and enraged about an imagined other and they see that imagined other coming to them, it is very possible for things to happen which are ugly, awful and lead to violence.

I think we need to respect the fact that road rage reflects the real rage of the driver at a situation usually beyond his or her control. We need also to remember that there are plenty of people who find a great deal of anxiety about what is going on in this time of change, when fluid boundaries make things unmanageable and unpredictable, in this time of conflict and of competing loyalites, in this new time. That anxiety is real, but negative othering, road rage, usually involves no respect for the other, no willingness to learn about the other, no willingness to engage the other to discover what things are shared, what things are not shared, what things you might work together on and what things you might oppose together. Negative othering involves attribution of motive to the other, motives which probably are not there, and for which you certainly have no evidence. Negative othering involves attributing intent, 'Oh, you intend to blow me up, or you intend to take over my society, or you plan to force me to follow your religious principles'. This attribution is often accompanied by a dehumanised view of the other, which enables all manner of negative things to be done out of self-defence.

Negative othering, like road rage, clearly involves the refusal of the right to share the road. The other does not have the right to be on the road; you alone have the right to be on the road, you can drive anywhere you want on the road, at any speed that suits you and heaven help the car that gets in your way, in the way of your superior purpose. Or you can drive a great big SUV down a road built for, well, a Morris Minor at best. The other does not exist. The other does not count. Road rage takes the day. Whether you consider yourself right or not, the other is clearly wrong. Moreover, road rage involves the denial that the road you are both on goes to the same place. We live in a time where these road rages go way past being funny. They crop up in neighbourhoods, in families, in national relations with each other, and they produce negative outcomes at each of those levels. Negative othering, like road rage, needs to be attended to carefully and called for what it is when it occurs. The antidote to road rage and negative othering is to call people together to engage with each other and to produce a set of experiences that are more human, and to nurture values and understandings that will produce a sustainable society. That is our challenge in the face of the road rage that threatens to destroy our societies.

Conclusion

Efforts to overcome diversity through driving out those who are different are doomed to failure in advanced modern industrial societies. Not only will they not produce unity, or even uniformity, the levels of repression required to achieve this and the dehumanising forms of negative othering involved will lead to unacceptable levels of social conflict. Those who call for the adoption of one way, the enshrining of their views in legislation designed to force others to comply, or who engage in negative othering to reduce diversity seem either unaware of the consequences of their approaches or willing to inflict/bear the cost. A cost few others are ready to pay. The reality of diversity and the changes this reality both reflects and demands make some feel weary, others fearful, and an increasing number attracted to the challenges is part of the emerging diversity.

Some Further Reading

Appleby, Scott, *The Ambivalence of the Sacred: Religion, Violence and Reconcilliation* (Lanham MD: Rowan & Littlefield, 2000).

Baumann, Zigmunt, *Liquid Fear* (Cambridge: Polity, 2006).

Carey, Hilary, *Believing in Australia* (Sydney: Allen and Unwin, 1996).

Cahill, Desmond, Gary Bouma, Hass Delall and Michael Leahey *Religion, Cultural Diversity and Safeguarding Australia* (Canberra: DIMIA, 2004).

Cimino, Richard, "'No God in Common:' American Evangelical Discourse on Islam After 9/11', in *Review of Religious Research*, 47, 2006: 162-174.

Hogan, Michael, *The Sectarian Divide: Religion in Australian History* (Melbourne: Penguin, 1987).

Thomas, Scott, *The Global Resurgence of Religion and the Transformation of International Relations: The Struggle for the Soul of the Twenty-first Century* (New York: Palgrave), 2005.

Chapter Three
Responses to Diversity–Snapping Along the Spandex–
Diversity and Social Cohesion

These chapters have been examining the challenges posed by religious diversity and approaches to its management. The facts of religious diversity in Canada, Australia and New Zealand were covered in the first chapter and the consequences of diversity in terms of boundary marking and inter-religious competition or conflict—the forms of 'road rage' that can exist between, or happen between groups as they travel together along the highway to Heaven.

This chapter takes up the issue of the challenge of religious diversity to social cohesion. Historically there has been a great variety of social policy aimed at reducing religious conflict in societies. The question before us is, 'Can a society like New Zealand is becoming hold together? Can societies like Australia, or like other multi-faith and multicultural societies which are becoming increasingly diverse continue to be productively diverse, or will they be torn apart by conflict? Will the centre hold or will it all fly apart? Will the rising religious diversity so stretch the social fabric that even the spandex snaps and it all gives way?'

We hear a lot of social fabric imagery and that is the image that shapes this chapter. How great is the threat of religious diversity to social cohesion? Can the fabric of society, of social order cope with the intensity of religious diversity that is emerging? The previous chapter made it clear that religious diversity is a serious problem not only to societies but also to religious groups themselves. Can religious groups hold together as their internal belief, ritual, and ethical diversities become more and more apparent and harder to manage? Does the society hold? Does the religious group hold? Such questions are becoming more salient as the challenges, worries and concerns seem ever to multiply as diversity manifests itself in all aspects of our life including religion. Will the social fabric hold, will the centre hold or will diversity fuelled conflict and competition lead to terrorism, violence, the breakdown of society, social order resulting in all of those horrific images that are seen in those disaster movies which are so popular amongst us where everything breaks down and all that is left is warring gangs fighting over the scraps of life as we know it now? Why people flock to these disaster movies I do not pretend to know but they do scare us a lot and we seem to like that. Disaster movies give us images of what happens when the social fabric gives way and conflict overpowers social order and cooperation, when those values required to sustain society no longer guide us.

Defining Social Cohesion

Defining social cohesion presents a very interesting problem. A review of sociological texts reveals that definitions of social cohesion are rare. Books on the social policy of social cohesion provide lists of factors that are necessary for a social democracy to hold together but not definitions of social cohesion. I think that what we mean by social cohesion is the following:

> social cohesion is quite simply the capacity of a society or a group to so organise its resources and people to produce what it needs to sustain and reproduce itself.

Societies require the production and consumption of goods and services along with sufficient reproduction of population, culture and knowledge so as to support, nurture and enhance life. This definition does not claim that it is necessary to maintain this or that particular feature of the society but argues that many particular arrangements, social structures, can and historically have provided what is needed for a society to produce and reproduce itself. Concerns for social cohesion rightly presume that internal conflict undermines the capacity of a society, group or organisation to do these things.

Types of Social Cohesion

This definition raises the question of what holds the society together and on this there are some very interesting arguments. We are very familiar with the first approach that asserts that a society will hold together if we are all the same. As the old aphorism goes, 'birds of a feather, flock together'. Sameness reduces conflict and confusion about purpose and orders of importance. Being the same. However, the call for sameness, begs the question, 'Being the same what?' This question stands at the core of all the arguments about multiculturalism, about multi-faith societies, and about will migration so change New Zealand, or Australia as to become unrecognisable.

One quick response is that members of a successful society must subscribe to similar values? Okay, so for social cohesion we must value roughly the same things, have similar aims, and pursue similar goals. I find it interesting that when you look at different societies and read research project after research project demonstrates that human groups and humans basically want the same things—jobs, some food, adequate shelter, education for their kids, health, and welfare. We all want the same things. There was a landmark study conducted in the United States of America in the 1940's by a Swedish academic called Gunnar Myrdal.

He was concerned about whether blacks and whites wanted the same things. Those opposed to racial integration argued that different races had different values. However, contrary to this opinion Myrdal discovered that they did hold the same values, Moreover he discovered that whites were most ready to give those things to blacks that blacks most wanted—education, access to jobs, and access to health services.

That study has been repeated hundreds of times over and over again with same results. One of my PhD candidates has just completed another one, this time in Australia and asking do Muslims want the same things as other Australian groups? Once again the answer is, 'Yes'. So there is that foundational similarity but it takes very different forms in different communities and so a new community can come in and join with others, because for the most part share they share the same values and concerns.

Others argue that we have to be the same ethnicity? Again, the question becomes, which ethnicity? Ethnicity, like race quickly becomes a big bad joke. Similar ethnicities, like we all should be British. What is British? As an ethnicity it is a great mélange of different waves of migration, invasion resulting in a mélange of different groups—Picts, Celts, Scots, Danes, and others—which have warred against each other from time to time. We have fought vigorously against each other and yet we are all British. Of course, I am not accepted in Australia, being an American. What a testimony to multi-culturalism the label 'British' is. How about the argument that we need to be the same race for a society to hold together? We all know that the concept of race is nonsense, an artificially and arbitrarily constructed division among people, a figment of the imagination of one group that wishes to dominate other groups through repression.

Then there are those that argue that we all need to be the same religion for a society to hold together. While religious conflict can tear a society apart, and the example of Ireland haunts us, Australians and New Zealanders have never been the same religion. New Zealanders had Presbyterians and Catholics and Methodists and Baptists, and now a few Muslims and Jews along with others, but it has not fallen apart. Australia has been religiously diverse for over 50,000 years and since European settlement has never had just one religion, nor has one denomination of Christianity comprised more than half the population. This diversity has not produced social order destroying conflict, has not pulled the society apart or prevented this society from producing and reproducing. So the idea that similarity is required for social cohesion quickly falls apart upon closer examination. We share a great deal as human beings. We have similar aims and goals, although we may have very different ways of packaging, celebrating and inculcating these things we share.

What holds a society together? A second proposed basis for social cohesion points to the role of structures of social control and power in organising the resources and energies of a society to achieve production and re-production. Here is where I part company with much of the current discussion of social cohesion in the policy think tanks of Western liberal democracies, which seem to presume that only democracies can enjoy social cohesion.

History provides many examples of societies that were very much held together by other, non-democratic, forms of government, or shapes of power organisation. There is nothing more socially cohesive than a really good dictatorship. North Korea is socially cohesive if nothing else. Divine right monarchies in the seventeenth and eighteenth centuries and totalitarian regimes in the twentieth held the society together by carefully and strictly regulating and ensuring production and re-production. The Chinese Communist Party rules China with an iron fist, limiting diversity, imposing their views with military force. Given the diversities produced and required for industrialisation the question becomes how long will they be able to do this? The capacity of the Nazis and Mussolini to organise production and run the trains on time did appeal to some in Britain and France who argued that, 'This place is getting out of control. We ought to have good social control, economic control; yes, we need structure, structures of power, and the capacity to coerce conformity.'

The echoes of this argument are heard in the 'law and order' arguments of some right-wing politicians today. Those who promote or accept this argument today forget that while strongly coercive central government approaches to social order provide a form of social cohesion which can be shown to work, such coercive and repressive totalitarian structures may last for a while, but then they fall apart. People revolt against the repression. The massive costs of repressive structures become unsupportable and uneconomical.

It simply cannot be denied that strong centralised forms of social control do provide a form of social cohesion. Singapore provides an example of a well-managed society and economy, which encompasses and harnesses diversities. Such approaches often get dismissed pretty early on today, because it is not a form that appeals to us. In that case it becomes appropriate to ask, 'What is the form of social cohesion producing social structure that we would like?' We usually say that we prefer the agreed processes we associate with democracy. The United States is trying forcefully to export democracy around the world, with limited success. But structures of power and control are important for holding a society together. There is no society without them. Given the necessity of structures and coercive legal frameworks, the question becomes, what kinds of structures. Citizens of liberal democracies tend to prefer agreed processes and responsible bureaucracies. Bureaucracies are structures of communication and decision making designed to achieve certain things for a group. We may laugh at them and poke fun at them but they do indeed hold societies together enabling and regulating production and reproduction.

There is a third approach to social cohesion. There is another way societies hold together, another form of social cohesion, one that actually depends on diversity, that is, social cohesion based on interdependence. I earlier made reference to the old aphorism, 'birds of a feather flock together'. However, there is another aphorism that declares that, 'opposites attract'. So much for aphoristic approaches to social theory! Common sense is often shown to be contradictory nonsense. The role of interdependence in social cohesion was identified by the French sociologist Emil Durkheim and the way interdependence works to produce social cohesion became increasingly clear in the twentieth century as societies became more diverse in a whole variety of ways—ethnically, religiously, and through various other kinds of cultural differences. As diverse societies emerged it became clear that the several parts to this diversity actually needed each other, they had become interdependent. In so far as they had become interdependent it was not possible or, perhaps more importantly, it was not profitable to seek to drive one or another out. Conflict was costly.

The logic of interdependence and social cohesion is quite simple. If we were did all the same things and produced the same things; if we were each self sufficient communities, for example, small subsistence farmers that did not have to sell anything to keep going, we could pretty well do without each other and the rest of the world. We could grow our food, we could eat our food, we could raise our family as so long as there was a little bit more land we could encourage our children to farm we could actually go on for a generation or two until we ran out of land. But that kind of self-sufficiency model has fallen apart and no longer obtains in diverse societies. For diverse urban societies there is no greater symbol of interdependence than when the garbage collectors go on strike. We need them, whoever they are, or the whole place stinks and becomes disease prone. Urban life is absolutely dependent on social cohesion grounded in interdependence. Without diversity cities die.

I have a wonderful cartoon that draws on inter-dependence for its humour. It shows this person sitting in a very gentlemanly type chair, reading his newspaper and his eyebrows are flaring up and he is looking terrified as he reads the headlines of the newspaper which declare, 'Nation in Peril—Sociologists on Strike'. But do you really need sociologists? This question tests the limits of interdependence. However, for the most part, we actually do need each other. We need occupational differentiation in order to get all the jobs done. We need professional differentiation to provide all the services we need and want. There are towns in Victoria and New South Wales that are pleading with the Australian government to let in the refugees in large numbers and assist them to settle in rural towns because their numbers will save those towns socially and financially, by providing employment, providing sufficient population to keep the banks open, the schools open, the medical clinics open. Migrant numbers are needed to do the jobs that other Australians are unwilling to do—work in abattoirs, harvesting fruit and vegetables, and manual labour.

The simple fact of our inter-dependence provides the foundational social cohesion in current multi-faith, multicultural societies. We cannot live without group x. That was learned the hard way in the twentieth century as some nations figured they could and then at their peril discovered they really could not. Today the American Southwest is finding out the hard way that their economies are hugely dependent on illegal Latino immigrants.

Challenges to Social Cohesion

Are there challenges to social cohesion? Yes, a quick glance around the world provides ample evidence of diversities that are challenging societies. Differences among people and groups do stretch the social fabric, and at times they do make things difficult. These challenging diversities can be ethnic, cultural, religious, and others. Societies today are experiencing the increased presence of various forms of diversity do to the global movement of people, cultures and capital. Moreover, western societies have become less equal and concerns are raised over challenges to social order based on differences in economic divisions and class. Where there is too great a differentiation in income, wealth, or social class there will be people who feel they must revolt or fight in order simply to get a living. The riots over changes in the welfare and retirement benefits, seen in France during 2010, stem from economic diversity, not religious or cultural diversity. Now New Zealand and Australia have had pretty good foundations placed in a welfare state system to see to it that the distribution did not get too great. However, the last twenty years has seen a considerable stretching of the social fabric as higher incomes have gone sky rocketing up and lower incomes have not kept up at all.

Differential access to the good things of life may produce challenges to social cohesion, may produce inter-group conflict, group tensions, inter-group competition within a society as deprived groups feel blocked from access to jobs, education, health or social services. If the differences that make a difference to access to the good things of life focus on religious differences then these differences can become very much a threat to social cohesion.

Take Ireland as a key example where social cohesion was very much shredded by conflict over Protestant vs Catholic group loyalties and allegiances. Each group was denied access to jobs, services and civic participation by the other. Another example is provided by India where at the moment Hindu nationalism is threatening to raise, there is the spectre on the horizon of a whole variety of discrimination and occasional violence based on religious differentiation. The aim of some is to make India a Hindu nation and to exclude Muslims, Sikhs and others. The recent violent conflict that beset Sri Lanka over recent years has been driven by Buddhists who said we want to have a Buddhist nation and we will drive out the others. Take another example, Myanmar, which is doing roughly the same thing. Yes these are Buddhist nations. I find it amusing that some people think that Buddhists cannot do anything wrong and could not be associated with violence or unjust practices. However, here are undeniable examples of Buddhist violence in those two places and this needs to be remembered.

Any group that gets itself associated with trying to purify the nation, another example of 'ethnic cleansing', like has happened in Sri Lanka, is happening in Myanmar, and threatens to happen in India can have very serious effect as people move toward. 'We must be alike, we must have a nation that is a Hindu nation, a Buddhist nation, a Christian nation, a Presbyterian nation, whatever you wish.' Then you get conflict because the unilateral association of national and religious identities and symbols by one group results in others not feeling welcome, but excluded, marginalised and threatened. When this happens social cohesion begins to be stretched to the snapping point. So is religious diversity a threat? Well, some say, 'Yes' and point to the fact that from 1648 the peace of Westphalia brought an end to the European wars of religion by enforcing religious singularity for each state. Europeans often say, 'Yes', religion produced violence and strife. This only ended when Europe agreed to divide the religions according to the state, on the basis of the principle—*cuius regio, eius religio* (literally, whose realm, his religion)—which meant that whatever religion the head of state was, the nation was and that religion would be the only religion and the followers of other religions needed to convert, get out, get over it, and become alike, or else. In this way. European religions became accustomed to having a monopoly status as state churches. Catholics in France, Anglicans in England, Presbyterians in Scotland from time to time have had monopoly status and they would say, 'we do not want that monopoly status changed because it produces very comfortable relationship with the state under which we thrive'. They also argued that this arrangement was the 'will of God' and must be maintained so that each group will be able to produce a healthy, happy society. European history, read in this way, clearly indicated that societies could not cope with religious diversity without social policies that repress diversity and favour one group over another.

Managing Diversity

The challenges of religious diversity to social cohesion make clear that the issue raised by diversity is how diversity is managed. Is diversity managed by law, social policy and regulation to promote mutual respect and understanding or is it used as a basis for conflict. Diversity itself is not a problem, but it can quickly be turned into a problem by those who would force the society toward a mono-cultural view of itself, or who use it as a way to distribute access to the good things of life in an inequitable manner, or to deny legitimacy to a section of the society. Inter-group hostility and violence in the past is very much what hangs behind a lot of the current European debates about social cohesion and which groups can be accommodated and which cannot. States that have been accustomed to religious singularity also find the arrangement convenient. All the head of government has to do is make one phone call to the moderator, to the bishop, or to whomever else is the leader of the one religion and connection has been made with the group. An office of religious affairs might well look after the interests of the religious group, ensuring that competition was held at bay, that salaries of clergy were paid, that theological education supported the interests of the state, and that pronouncements by religious leaders were acceptable. Such an office would probably also look after internal diversity, identifying and punishing heretics and ensuring uniformity of practice.

What looms behind much of the argument about social cohesion in Western societies is 'Islamophobia'; fear of Islam. There is a fear of that particular religious group, fear that Muslims will do things that will injure the society, things that will change it in ways other members of the society fear they will not like. I find it very interesting that in the mid 1990s Pauline Hanson in Australia was worried about Asians. She did not express any concern about Muslims in the 1990s but, after 9/11 2001, the 'other' about whom to be fearful shifted from Asians to Muslims. It is helpful to remember that there is always an 'out' group, there has usually been a group that we are supposed to be worried about.

The neat thing about Australian history, and I suspect its true also about Canada and New Zealand as well, is that if you go back in time you will discover different groups in the past that were the ones that were going to be the hard ones to ingest and the hard ones to settle and who were going to be difficult. Australia had a lot of trouble with Irish for a while, Catholics like Muslims today were considered incapable of learning to live in democratic countries, and not sufficiently rational to succeed in high level appointments. Then there were other groups, the Greeks; they were a bit of a challenge to social cohesion and the Australian way of life in the early 1960's. An examination of many points in history reveals the same kind of xenophobic logic and stereotyping occurring as different groups were subject to 'negative mothering'. Concern about social cohesion is often about accommodating, working out an arrangement with, and negotiating the space with a more recently arrived group.

Is social diversity a threat to social cohesion? While many would answer, 'Yes', there is also a 'No' case as well. The great land now referred to as Australia has been religiously and culturally diverse for about 50,000 years. Aboriginal diversity in Australia provides an interesting case with literally hundreds of cultures, languages and religions. Yes, there were squabbles, there were fights but on the whole the thing held together pretty well. Diversity in Australia continued in European settlement. The first fleet was diverse. There are other examples of successful religiously diverse societies both in history and in the present. Examples include Andalusia where Catholics, Jews and Muslims worked together, sharing knowledge and producing art, Sicily where Roman Catholics, Greek Orthodox, Jews and Muslim lived harmoniously and productively. Contemporary Japan is an interesting case of religious diversity. Many Japanese are born Shinto, married Christian and buried Buddhist. Why not? That is an interesting way to negotiate diversity. I am told that this is because Japanese prefer or like the rites for each of those rites of passage provided by these different groups.

The United States is religiously diverse to a degree. China was religiously diverse in some ways until Mao and then religion was actively repressed and religious practice forbidden. Now China permits a short list of religions to operate. Canada has long had to manage Protestant vs Catholic diversity along with linguistic diversity. New Zealand with its bicultural civic policies, demographic religious diversity, and increasing cultural and ethnic diversity holds together because of arguments and deliberate programmes of inclusion, openness to welcome diversity, and a shared commitment to work together. This is also facilitated by economy that still needs additional labour and can absorb migrants.

Factors in the Management of Religious Diversity

There are some critical factors in the successful management of religious diversity. The three to be highlighted here are demographic, historical and cultural factors. The demographic factors are very important to look at in comparing the ways nations manage religious diversity. Given the presence of diversity, a key to understanding their relationships will be found in the number and relative size of the religious involved. If no group is, or has ever been able to dominate, you get a very different playing field than if one was dominant and is no longer or one is looking to become dominant, the 50%/50% situation is the worst place to be, 40%/40% is pretty grim too because each one thinks 51% is just around the corner. That whole ambition to being the dominant group is terribly important because with dominance comes responsibility. The question becomes if we are dominant what is our religious duty in terms of shaping the society? And what is our relationship with other groups? And how much space do we give and how much do we not give? Malaysia illustrates these issues quite clearly at the moment having just recently, in the last twenty or thirty years, gone over to 60% Muslim. Now being predominantly Muslim, Malaysia is trying to figure out what it means to be an Islamic state. In these ways, the demographic composition of a society is seen to be important to the way religious diversity is likely to be managed. Australia has many religious groups, as does New Zealand, with the result that no one group is demographically dominant, yet while cultural dominance may have accrued to one or two groups at the same time they could never have voted anybody else out.

There is an historical dimension to the management of religious diversity. Has there been violence between the groups in the past? If there has been historical violence between the groups in the society under consideration, then that historical memory of violence continues on and on for a long time. I find it very interesting how violence records itself in the memory of a group and lingers on for a long time. Take for example, my grandmother, saintly grandmother on my father's side. However, if you mentioned Catholics she would suddenly go into a rage. I mean, calm, compassionate Granny at all other times, but upon the mention of Catholics she would begin angrily spitting in Dutch, going on about, '*Philip de Tweede*, did we not know?' 'No, I didn't know about *Philip de Tweede*, I did not even know what those Dutch words meant.' Later I learned that Philip the Second of Spain, ran Holland rather brutally and the Catholics were rather brutal to the Protestants and my grandmother, who was a nice Dutch woman, stood very tall as Dutch women often do, had black curly hair which is not typically Dutch and so there might well have been some not entirely voluntary insertion of DNA into the family tree back there centuries ago. The memory of that may have been carried the form of anti-Catholic rhetoric and feeling so that 400 years later she is still raving on about *Philip the Tweede*. It is clear that one should be very careful about using violence; if you engage in it now the consequences are going to hang around for a long time!

On the other hand, we can ask whether there has been an experience of positive diversity. Is that part of the cultural memory of a place, the experience of a rich diversity which has been productive? Can, for example Spain call on the period of positive productive diversity of Andalusia to map a way forward to a positive appreciation of religious diversity in the twenty-first century following such a long period of the inquisition? I do not know whether this works, but Spain is working on promoting healthy inter-religious relations at this moment. So the historical and cultural factors in how 'difference' is constructed and what meanings are put on 'difference' are very important for the way religious diversity is negotiated in a society and whether it leads to violence or cooperation, mutual celebration or contestation.

When examining the conditions of social cohesion it is necessary to look at the way cohesion is working at several different levels—societal, sub-group and organisation. I am not going to do that throughout this chapter because it gets to be far too complex. For example at the societal level, the question becomes how does the society hold together? While at the sub-group or organisational level, the question becomes how do these sub-groups, or organisations hold together, achieve their goals and produce and reproduce themselves? Once several levels are examined it quickly becomes clear that there can be conflict between social cohesion at one level and social cohesion at another. For example, take a look at Ireland, there was nothing more cohesive than the Catholic and the Protestant sub-groups, but the society as a whole was a mess. Sub-group social cohesion, if it is antithetical to the other groups produces societal conflict but within group social cohesion.

I could again cite my own youth where we were Christian Reformed, they were only Reformed and there was a great deal of internal cohesion and a lot of competition, no violence, but each defining themselves over against the other made the internal cohesion strong. Similar processes occur between ethnic groups, ethnic neighbourhoods, and ethnic organisations. In-group solidarity often rolls over into competitiveness for example in sport and may lead to conflict. In my youth there was nothing more competitive than when Grand Rapids Christian High School played Catholic Central High School for the basketball title match.

What unites at one level might actually be disuniting at another. Managing social cohesion so that sub-group cohesion does not produce discord in the society can be difficult. Some groups have beliefs that they take to mean they have to be in conflict and that they have to try to impose their will and their way. In such cases you begin to get the erosion of social cohesion as one group or another seeks to impose its views upon those who do not share their views. It is the rare group that does not seek to shape society according to its views of how things should be. A review of some national examples may clarify some of the approaches and complexities involved in diversity management.

Some National Examples of Diversity Management

New Zealand has adopted a bi-cultural approach to the management of diversity and has developed the kinds of skills, policies and structures that have over time promoted the capacity to respect and honour difference among Maori and Pakeha. Can these abilities be extended to others or is biculturalism the norm and all other diversities merely tolerated as side issues? Ask Pacific Islanders about this as they begin to seek appropriate recognition, place and participation in their society. That is one of the current challenges.

Australia has basically practiced inclusion rather than exclusion, freedom rather than control and has a reasonably healthy relationship amongst most religious groups in the nation. That is being tested at the moment as some groups are demanding that their right to speak in negative ways about others is a religious right and so vilification becomes a religious right.

Meanwhile the United Nations deliberates a proposal from some Muslim states seeking to protect Islam and, grudgingly, other religions from defamation. While this seems to make sense in some countries it does not in Western liberal democracies where individuals, but not religions, are protected from defamation.

France and Turkey are quite different with their cultures of *laicité* in which no religious voice is allowed in the public sphere. No religious symbol is allowed in public offices. All schools, all legislatures, and agencies have non-religious bases, absolutely by constitutional definition. *Laicité* provides the cultural legitimation for recent legislation banning the wearing of the headscarf at schools and wearing other religious symbols in public spaces in France. You can wear such things outside the public space but you cannot wear them in public because that is a non-religious space, defined as such during the French Revolution, and reaffirmed in the early 1900's with all the implications now so publicly being worked out. This is a very interestingly different cultural arrangement that is hard to understand from other Western perspectives. This amounts to an absolute relegation of religion to the private sphere and a demotion of religion and religious voices to a place of deference to the state and the non-religious.

Denmark is still another case, where today 85% of Danish youth are confirmed in the eleventh year of high school. This is not historical; this is now. I emphasise 85% of Danish youth are confirmed, not just baptised, but also confirmed. They may never go to church but they are Christian. They identify themselves as Christian and see Danish society as a Christian society. Now if you happen to be a non-Christian in Denmark this form of Christian society becomes very interesting and powerfully excluding. All religious affairs in Denmark are controlled by the state church (the Danish Lutheran Church). But, let us say, I wanted to open an Anglican church in Denmark, to do so I would have to ask the Danish Lutheran Church for permission. They have actually given it to it so that there is an Anglican Parish in Copenhagen. But what if I were a Muslim, then I still have to ask the Danish Lutheran Church; or if I were from the Church of Scientology, I still would have to ask the Danish Lutherans and they will decide which groups are acceptable and which groups are not. They manage the list of who provides an acceptable form of religion in Denmark. I find this a very interesting case, which is almost unthinkable from the perspective of a society, which does not have a state church, or a governmental department of religious affairs. Sweden is similar in some ways and so is Finland. England, Denmark, and Sweden each have state churches to provide the 'normal' form of religion, but others must ask. For example in England if you happen to be a Methodist, Muslim or Buddhist chaplain you have to ask the Anglican chaplain for permission to visit 'your' people in prison.

Malaysia provides another example. In the past few decades it has become nearly 60% Muslim. The question is now being asked, what does it mean to be a Muslim country? There are many examples they could have chosen from and invented their own form. However, they invited a group of Wahabbists from Saudi Arabia who told them their strict and narrow views of what being a Muslim society meant, how shari'a law was to be implemented and interpreted. Malaysia might have invited people from across the straits whose culture is more similar to theirs and listened to Indonesians who have a very different view in these matters and a substantial history of doing it their way. Rather Malaysia has been following Wahabbist track. I find Wahabbism to be very similar to Calvinism—strict, doctrinaire, self-righteous, and prone to social engineering. Wahabbism is rather like Calvinism in its Cromwellian forms. Whatever, the question Malaysia is trying to answer is what does it mean to be a Muslim country?

These examples demonstrate that the management of diversity is done quite differently in different places. Anybody who says that a policy of separation of church and state covers the issues misses the huge diversity of the ways in which religion and the state are related in different societies. To invoke the separation of church and state opens up a wonderful door through which to look for more forms of diversity revealing a huge rainbow of different ways of doing it. There is no one 'way'. Take Fiji where the unofficial power of the Methodist Church forces the government to take actions that are detrimental to Hindus, Muslims and others. In other Pacific Island nations there are cases where a particular Christian group is trying to so define religious inter-group relations that only Christians may apply for recognition and in such a way that deems Mormons to be insufficiently Christian to be allowed to operate. In each of these cases a policy arrangement involving religion and the state is designed to favour one group and either to make things difficult or impossible for others.

Religious Voices in Secular Societies

Australia and New Zealand claim in some ways to be secular societies, yet they have a strongly Christian culture and demographically they are multi-faith. But as I have said, before secular does not mean irreligious. The understanding of the nature of a secular society is changing and increasingly a secular society refers to one that provides a very wide range of freedom of religion and belief, freedom to be religious, or not; freedom to choose among spiritualities and the freedom of non-belief. Secular societies do not privilege any religious group, nor those who hold to other perspectives. Neither Australia nor New Zealand has an official or state religion. In a very real sense religion and spirituality in these societies are out of control. The state does not seek to control religion and spirituality and it is becoming increasingly apparent to them that religious organisations are less and less able to control religion and spirituality, as the diversity within religious groups increases. A secular society is also one in which both religious and other than religious arguments are heard in social policy debates.

What this means for our civic space however is very interesting and is changing at the moment. It is this change that is catching some people out as religious voices are again heard alongside secular ones. Those seeking to promote or prevent a change in social policy, or health provision, or social service in a public space discussion—a civic forum, legislature, or policy seminar—are likely to discover that somebody now will either support or oppose their ideas from a religious perspective. That means that religious voices are re-entering the civic space in a different way in Australia and New Zealand. We have not been accustomed to explicitly religious arguments since about the end of the war in Viet Nam. Much of the protest against that war was religiously legitimated, religiously motivated and led by religious personnel. Yes there has been a kind of religious background to some discussions, but the Protestant voice became secularised from the late 1970s. Protestants lost their religious voice. In contrast, Catholics have not stopped being religiously articulate in the public policy domain taking positions that are usually a well grounded in their tradition.

But now there are new voices, which are coming up, voices that are explicitly religious. Emerging migrant communities from particular religious backgrounds argue for changes and developments in social policy to enable them to be faithful to their religious traditions in their adopted country. For example, Muslims have argued successfully for changes to the burial regulations. In this context new religious voices are emerging and calling themselves Christian voices. They are beginning to steal the show from other Christians because they are the only ones labeling themselves as Christian. With the liberal, compassionate Protestant voice secularised into non-existence the strident exclusivist voice of the Christian right is the only voice heard claiming the 'Christian' space in public discourse. This is particularly true when they are joined by conservative Catholic voices.

When a voice enters a public discourse from a religious point of view it changes the nature and context of the debate. Those who would seek to counter that voice must do so out of an explicitly named and carefully grounded value position. Quite simply, to counter one religious voice in a social policy debate, it is often necessary to speak out of another theologically grounded position, preferably from within the same tradition. A recognisably grounded philosophical position might well be respected as such. But in the public sphere, a religious voice, for example a voice claiming to represent Christians, is going to carry a certain weight unless it is qualified, or contradicted, by another religious voice, one, which is grounded in a different reading of the same Scriptures and theology. The exclusivist, negative, or conservative Christian voice will be the only one listened to, unless the compassionate inclusive Christian voice is also grounded in Scripture and theology in its expression in public policy debates. And so the liberal, compassionate and inclusive voice that does not ground itself in a theologically firm position does not get heard in the same way. This is what is new in the secular public forum and provides a very different context for the expression of religious voices in public policy debates. It calls for those who are religious to be theologically and scripturally articulate when speaking in public policy debates.

The form of a secular society emerging in Australia and New Zealand is not one where religious voices are pushed out of policy debates. However, when a religious voice enters the debate on one side of a debate, those who for religious reasons take a different view must use a religious voice to argue their case in order for it to be effective. For example, this has become apparent in attempts to develop counter terrorism programs. Those nations that are attempting to argue against that minority of Muslims who produce a theologically grounded argument in favour of violence against the West, are finding that an important part of the answer is a well grounded Muslim theology that says that violence against innocents is wrong. The answer to religiously motivated violence is not economic aid. It is not the job of Western, or Christian scholars to produce such a theology. The good news is that it is being produced as Muslim scholars revisit the core of Islam, draw deeply on the themes of justice and compassion and speak out firmly against violence. This is being very effective in counter terrorist activities around the world. A theological argument that says, 'No, violence does not work, that to engage in violence against innocents is not Qur'anic.'

So the theological contestation in public policy debates in a secular society like Australia is now calling on people to name their value positions and if somebody says, 'I am a Christian and think that . . .' and they are the only ones in the room that are willing to say that then that voice becomes THE Christian voice. And if that voice does not include the voice of compassion, then those of us who take a more inclusive view are left out of the debate, and our views do not count. The management of religious diversity becomes interesting and challenging in multi-faith societies as religious voices contest with each other and with voices grounded in other value bases.

A Case Study: Church Supports Civil Unions for Same Sex Couples

As part of the lecture series in Wellington, we held a 'spirited conversation' in a Wellington pub one night. Even though it was Queen's Birthday Public Holiday Monday and the pub was not planning to be open over sixty people attended and a VERY lively conversation ensued. Part of it went as follows—pardon the verbatim, but it keeps the liveliness of the occasion.

LLOYD GEERING: I just wanted to go back a wee bit to the dialogue just before this and to your pointing out that the progressive Christian voice, if there is such a thing, was not being heard whereas the more conservative Christian voice is being heard, that sort of thing. There is a problem here. And the problem is this. As you and I agreed the word 'religion' has negative connotations in society today. What we have not realised is that the word 'Christian' also has negative connotations. Now, I can remember the time that near the beginning of the twentieth century, when if you had said to anybody in New Zealand that you were not a Christian you would have offended them. It did not mean that they went to church, but of course they would affirm Christian values. But today, if you say to a person you are a Christian they might very well be offended, because the word 'Christian' has become associated with the fundamentalist voice. They are the ones who are claiming to be THE Christians. Now against that background we have to ask ourselves, if we put in a voice for compassion and justice, do we have to claim it is a Christian voice? My point is that the claim for compassion and justice stands on its own merits and that is why those of us who are in a sort of vaguely progressive church, or vaguely progressive stream of Christianity should not be over worried whether what we say is Christian or not. The question is this, is it compassion, is it justice and if so, that enables us to join forces with everybody in the community who may be Atheist, Agnostics or Buddhists or whatever, those who are also concerned with compassion and justice? It is the values that really matter not where you think they came from. Anyway I would want to argue that wherever they came from in New Zealand have they come from Christianity?

GARY BOUMA: I am afraid that I must disagree with you Lloyd and I will tell you why. I disagree with both the desirability to not label and the notion that by labeling you cut yourself off from the capacity to work with others. In 1982, later Archbishop (then later occasionally Governor General Peter Hollingworth), was then head of the Brotherhood of St Lawrence, and made precisely the argument that Lloyd has just made. He claimed that we argue on the basis of universal values, our proposals stand on their own merit and we will bring together more people this way than if we call these things Christian and work them out of our theology. The Brotherhood of St Lawrence still holds to that view and I have ceased giving them money as a result, because nobody is raised with universal values, Hans Kung to the contrary notwithstanding, and few are motivated by them. We have values and as Lloyd Geering says if these values are compassionate in New Zealand and Australia they probably stem somewhere from Christianity. However, to cut ourselves off from that well spring is to cut ourselves off from its motivational strength, it is to cut off from the source, is to cut off from the basic story, is to cut off values from substance. I argue.

For example, I was in Yogyakarta at a meeting of the <u>Nahdlatul Ulama</u> (President Abdurrahman Wahid) Gus Dur's group, representing forty million Muslim Indonesians and they were working toward an interfaith statement designed to legitimate involvement in interfaith activities. And they came up with a really fine statement and each proposition was grounded in the Qur'an and the Hadith in the great traditions of Islam and somebody said, 'Look, we should take those citations out because the arguments stand by themselves. We will have more people standing with us'. And I said, 'No, let the world show where Islamic theology takes you. Which would you rather have, a denatured statement from Yogyakarta about interfaith, or one that comes directly and profoundly out of the religious values held by two hundred million Indonesians?'

We can see this more clearly in an overseas case, but it is equally true at home. Take for instance, the Australian Christian Lobby which is a very effective lobby group who have claimed for themselves the label, 'Christian', and if allowed to continue in this way in about ten more years no one else will be able to use this label as they will have totally monopolised it. Unless, of course, somebody stands up and says, 'Sorry, we too are Christian and we take a very different view of these matters than you do, FOR SCRIPTURAL AND THEOLOGICAL REASONS'. Unless 'we too' have a lobby group which is not just, 'Oh, bishop so and so talked to such and such a politician'. Yes, that is the way it used to go. The archbishop would call the prime minister, the prime minister would call the archbishop, the values would worked on would be done so through informally, with no problem whatsoever, and no one had to say anything about Christianity. However, that is not the way it works now. Every lobby group has its own particular value basis in a particular ideology or theology about which they are more or less explicit.

I find that I can work with Muslims much more easily if I am theologically clear as a Christian and they say, 'Oh yes, we have religiously motivated compassion too, can we come alongside because we know your compassion springs from your beliefs. Mine springs from mine. Let us stand together and be strong because we are deeply grounded each in our own traditions and that position is not likely to be swept away by opposition.'

It is enlightenment, triumphalism that says the universal values will take us through. They will not, since they are not universal, moreover, they have failed to provide an adequate foundation for the discipline and sacrifice required to achieve the adoption and practice of compassion and inclusion in social policies. They are not holding in the current crisis. If they were, we would not be having these crises. So, I am sorry Lloyd, I wish I could agree with you, but I cannot.

The Rev Dr Margaret Mayman (Senior Minister of the St Andrew's Presbyterian Church). *I want to give an example of how that has worked for us. One of the things that we have been involved in at St Andrews Church was around supporting the Civil Union Legislation, As a Parish Council we made a submission to the Parliamentary Select Committee on this matter and I thought well, you know, this is a Select Committee, New Zealand is a secular state, thus we needed to make sure that we grounded our St Andrew's statement in language that people who are not Christian could understand. So we worked really hard at putting it into human rights language. But once we got into the interview, the sort of meeting part of the Select Committee, the first person who asked us a question was a fundamentalist Christian member of parliament who quoted a biblical verse—one of the Leviticus verses. Because we are compassionate and inclusive Christians, ones who have been dealing with sexuality issues, have gone through those texts in Leviticus, and we understand that they are so often taken out of context, I was able to respond in a way that, explained what was going on in that text. The liberal non-Christian members of the Select Committee who wanted to support gay relationships and civil unions were so excited that they asked, 'Can you do that for those other verses in the Bible because there is this one and this one and this one'. And so they asked us to make a supplementary submission that was a biblical and theological perspective in support of the case we were making for the introduction of civil unions and eventually for Gay marriage. So, our second submission was 'out-there' Christian and I was really surprised that it was needed. But, it helped me understand that we do actually have something to offer from our faith tradition, that which we stand in, within this wider community. And I think particularly as I have got to know other people of other faiths more and more I am realising that if you want to participate in multi-faith encounters, you actually have to be*

able to stand secure in knowing who you are. It is from that point you can-
not engage with others from a universal point of view because that is kind
of making Christianity universal and that is what our fore bearers did. We
have to actually say this is what is particular about who we are and what we
have to offer and it is amazing the things that will flow from those conversa-
tions.

The new social policy discourse requires that people name their value bases and that they argue coherently from their value base for the policies they support. Increasingly those policies will have to support diversity in many areas of life including religious diversity. What this means for social cohesion is not always clear. There will be times when a society says that in order for us to hang together, we may have to limit this or that. So in coping with religious diversity there are some cultural issues, some societal issues, and some personal level issues. We have to look at our culture and how it understands diversity because we are moving away from a set of assumptions about mono-culturalism to multi-culturalism, 'isms' in the sense of ideologies, beliefs and assumptions about diversity. Many of us, and many of our leaders, still have lingering in our minds the whole notion that mono-culturalism is best and that we will get there someday if we just hang around and shake this bag of cats long enough so that they will get to be cooperative. But Australia and New Zealand are no longer mono-cultural, if they ever were. Being demographically multicultural, multiculturalism—positive beliefs and values about diversity including religious diversity is clearly the way of the future.

In this context the question becomes, 'Do we have theologies of diversity which enable people to understand religious diversity as God given?' How do we incorporate and include many religions in a way that keeps the social fabric together but enables people to do those things that are important to them? And there are very interesting work place related issues that come up about when you seek to accommodate different religious timetables, calendars, symbols, clothing and practices.

One European nation proposed the following solution. To solve the problems raised by people needing different blocks of time off for religious and spiritual reasons, we will simply give everybody x number of days off in the year and they can take them whenever it suits them for whatever reason they want, we do not care whether it is religious, personal or whatever and that is the way it will be. So there are ways of managing diversity but the issues are there and not always easy. How are we to accommodate religious diversity in such a way that the society can produce what it needs, people can do what they need to do and it all works out productively in the end? If the goal is productivity and sustainability, then creative ways forward can be found. If the goal is to somehow, keep a particular pattern of holidays, to favour one group over another or to maintain a particular form of associations, then the task may be harder to achieve. Civic life, holidays, marking tragedies, celebrations, may need to be done in a variety of different ways. And at a personal level one may be called upon to choose how to relate to others and to work that out, but again those decisions have to be coordinated in ways that work toward promoting social cohesion by promoting inclusion and supporting the capacity to produce and reproduce.

There are two basic approaches to diversity; you can either be inclusive or exclusive. If you take the path of inclusion you will move toward positive outcomes time and time again according to increasing amounts of data now available. If you promote participation in the society you get people who feel part of it, feel committed to it, are ready to be productive within it, are ready to sacrifice for it, and will see their future as tied up in the wellbeing of the society. Inclusivity enhances economic productivity as more people become involved in economic cooperation. Social inclusion promotes other forms of cooperation and as social cohesion is enhanced the society becomes a place that is attractive to others. We will explore social policy strategies of exclusion and inclusion.

Strategies of Exclusion

Social policies of exclusion, uniformly lead to negative outcomes. Social scientists have known this for a long time and wonder why it is that many still find policies of exclusion appealing. Some react positively when political leaders decide, 'Oh we have to be exclusive in this way or that'. Exclusion produces people who are bitter, who are envious, prone to conflict, likely to withdraw from the society, become less willing to participate, are less able to be connected, thus weakening the social fabric so that the networks do not hold people together. Those excluded do feel that they are part of the society. If they are not part of it they may feel quite satisfied to do something to bring it down.

Exclusion is a very costly social exercise. It leads to enclaves, despair, to violence and forces those excluded to adopt survival kinds of responses. And if you are in a survival mode you will do things you never thought you would do in your life. You become willing to sacrifice others, self and resource and do things you would never do before if it is deemed necessary to survive.

There are a variety of strategies of exclusion. You will hear them proposed from time to time. Some societies practice exclusion by declaring a group to be illegal. Scientology was declared illegal in Australia for a while. Witchcraft is still illegal in some Australian states. Another way to exclude a group is to declare that following it is unhealthy, it is not good for you to be x. It is very interesting to look at that kind of argument. There are some really nasty things happening in terms of cult repression in Europe at the moment. Many Europeans states have ministries of religion, which maintain a short list of okay religions, a longer list of not so hot religions, and a list of those that they are actively repressing because they are unhealthy. France recently passed a law that said made it illegal to 'exploit a person's weakness'. At first this sounds good. I would not want to exploit a person's weakness, no, that's not fair, it is not good. However, the law was aimed at those cults, according to the cult control agencies, who exploit a spiritual weakness. As with much legislation, the issue becomes where do you draw the line? As a result of the legislation in fact now some psychotherapists are being brought in and brought up on charges of exploiting a person's weakness and pastoral counseling is under attack.

Another exclusivist strategy involves the formal recognition of one or a few religions. China is interesting. It recognises seven or eight, up to ten depending on how you count. For example, Protestants and Catholics are two different religions because they use different Chinese names for God. They are both okay so long as they each use the form recognised by the state. But if your religion is not on the approved list you will be subject to terrible things and repression. The best known example is the Falun Gong. Russia too has a short list. In Russia your religion had better have been recognised by the state before about 1912. If you were not a recognised religion by 1912 you have little chance of gaining recognition in Russia today.

And then there is a sort of informal exclusion strategy that is found in the saying, 'Well that is just not us'. This would be the effect of those who strive to have Australia declare itself to be 'Christian society'. The effect of this is to make all non-Christians feel excluded. Even taking the proposal seriously has the effect of exclusion. One form this strategy takes is to propose policies restricting migration by denying certain groups permission to enter the country. Some 'Christian' groups in Australia ask 'Why do not we stop Muslim migration?' I did a study that explored social distance and religious groups in Australia. Social distance was measured by a series of questions for each of eight groups running from 'Welcome group X as a member of the family' to 'keep out of the country'. It was amusing to see how a national sample of Australians would respond to this study. The least accepted group was the Jehovah's Witnesses. However, Muslims attracted the most who responded that they should be kept out of the country entirely. Anglicans were by a statistically significant difference the most likely to give this response among major Australian religious groups. This reflects a current practice of negative othering and strategies of exclusion engaged in my some Anglicans.

Strategies of exclusion include preventing a religious group from building a place of worship, opening faith based schools or participating in civic events. The newspapers are full of reports of these activities. What is less often reported are the many occasions of inclusion that occur in Australia and New Zealand daily.

Strategies of Inclusion

There are strategies of inclusion as well. Fortunately this is a longer list and one that actually is easier to work. A key strategy to inclusion and the development of a successful multi-faith society is education about religions. Australia has no education about religion in the school curriculum. We get secularism going strong in the schools, but nothing informative about religion to counter ignorance. Every time I work with a minority religious group in Australia they say, 'Oh tell people about us so that they know who we are, where we come from, where we fit. The level of religious ignorance is driving us crazy.' I think education about world religions is terribly important. It is needed to overcome the fears and misapprehensions that come from ignorance of religions, both our own and those of others. We have forms of ethnic diversity education in the schools, so we hear about various ethnic groups, but what about religious diversity? This too is an important part of our society and an important dimension of our lives. Part of educating about world religions involves educating the media. Most young reporters have little idea about any religion; often not having one themselves are unable to understand the religious or the spiritual in others. Thus, the most important strategy of inclusion is to provide education about religions.

The second major strategy of social inclusion is to promote inter-religious relations, promoting dialogue, and inter-group respect. I was part of the organising team for the Parliament of the World's Religions held in Melbourne in 2009. I have been very much involved in the Council of Christians and Jews. The Gulen movement in Australia has been most active in bringing Australians of various religious backgrounds together with Muslims over meals so that they have a social evening, whereby they are learning about each other, demystifying each other, and sharing stories. While most often held during the fasting month of Ramadan, they sponsor many events where ordinary Australians can get together, acknowledge their religious differences and yet share a social space and come away feeling connected across the differences. The interactions in these events are interesting as each learns something about the other. As people get to know each other the quality of the conversations moves from polite to authentic. These interfaith relations are terribly important in terms of building relationships among people across lines of religious, the lines of religious difference.

A third strategy of social inclusion involves civic inclusion. Civic inclusion, involvement in politics, policy making, public forums, and inclusive language use are each terribly important in making any group, including religious groups seen to be part of the society and involved in the running of the nation. Symbolic and representational involvement is very important to civic inclusion. If religious symbols are present in a civic space, then may they not just be of one tradition. Holding of community events in the religious premises of one group, say an Anglican Cathedral, poses problems even if statements of inclusion are made. The Melbourne inter-religious service to mark the events of September 11 were held in the Rod Laver Tennis Arena. It was packed. Each religious group was given five minutes. It was grandly colourful and left all with a feeling of being included. If events are opened with the prayers of one group, the prayers of many should be included. This practice should be adopted by those parliaments currently opened with the recitation of the Christian Lord's Prayer.

Community policing is part of civic inclusion. While ethnic and religious profiling of suspects is highly excluding and productive of resentment, those places that have invested in community policing, building relationships between police and various groups in the society are major factors in promoting social inclusion. I have been working with the police in the State of Victoria where we have a Multi-faith Police Advisory Group to help the police understand and work with communities.

It works a treat. The evidence for this is the fact that those who turned in the radical jihadist groups who were planning attacks in Australia were Muslims, members of the Muslim community who did not like what was going on. Because the police had set up very good police community relations, community members trusted the police. Community members and leaders also knew what to do with their concerns. This would never have happened without good community policing.

A fourth strategy of social inclusion involves promoting cultures of inclusion. Cultures that are difference accepting, not denying differences among us (for we are not all the same), are accepting that there are real differences. Many of these differences make for a more interesting world, while others of them are more challenging. We need cultures that enable one to accept the fact that all people are different in some ways and consider that desirable; cultures that make it clear that we all need each other and cultures that enable us to even value that difference. It is important because it adds a richness to our society, increasing our ability to cope and develop more creative solutions than if we all thought the same way. Theologies of inclusion are required in the rejection of exclusivism, which claims that we are the only ones, or in rejecting supercessionism, which claims you may be marginally alright, but we are much better. Theologies that declare that that difference is intended, is a good in itself. One starting point is to remember what we have learned from our studies of nature that difference in itself is good, that bio-diversity is essential to a healthy environment.

Finally, there are strategies of pragmatic inclusion—an approach that says, this works for me, and that works for you. It also argues that through discussion and conversation people with different religious and values foundations can often agree on practical projects and on the shape their society should take. Their agreements will never be absolute, someone or some group will always disagree, but tentative commitments to projects and policies can be made, tried and assessed. Pragmatic coincidence of interests and aims will go quit a way in promoting social cohesion and cooperative productivity.

Conclusion

So diversity is needed, socially, societies that are all the same would be boring, not sustainable, and not survivable. Diversity is essential to advanced modern societies. Societies do not need similarity for social cohesion. Social cohesion derives from and relies upon interdependence. What is necessary for social cohesion is the full realisation that we need each other. A society does itself a great injury when it thinks it can do without this or that group and moves to exclude or eliminate them. The Germans learned that with respect to Jews and need to learn again with respect to Turkish Muslims. So those in the USA learn when they seek to oust and no longer admit Latinos. Miami could not survive without Haitian and Cuban refugees. Israel needs Palestinian labour and markets. Rural towns in Victoria, like Cobden, Mildura and Seymour need migrants, including Muslim refugees. The list could go on.

In highly differentiated urban societies and increasingly all others, we need each other. We need to cooperate in order to enable the society to produce and reproduce. But we do need some structures that enable respectful conversations as we share our different perspectives in shaping a way forward. We need structures to hold us together, to affirm our interdependence and to restrain those who would go it alone or would eliminate the others. Diversity also requires each group to be articulate about who they are, what they stand for and why. Successful diversity requires each group to draw on its own traditions and deep spiritual wells to make its contribution to the whole.

Some Further Reading

Beyer, Peter, *Religions in Global Society* (London: Routledge, 2006).

Fergusson, David, *Church, State and Civil Society* (Cambridge: Cambridge University Press, 2004).

Jupp, James, John Nieuwenhuysen and Emma Dawson (editors) *Social Cohesion in Australia* (Melbourne: Cambridge University Press, 2007).

Jupp, James (editor) *The Encyclopedia of Religion in Australia* (Melbourne: Cambridge University Press, 2009).

Myrdal, Gunnar, *An American Dilemma* (New York: Harper and Brothers, 1994).

Pew Forum, *Global Restrictions on Religion.* Accessed December 12, 2010, http://pewforum.org/Government/Global-Restrictions-on-Religion.aspx

Richardson, James (editor) *Regulating Religion: Case Studies from around the Globe* (New York: Kluwer/Plenum, 2004).

Wright-Neville, David and Anna Halafoff (editors) *Terrorism and Social Exclusion; Misplaced Risk: Common Security* (Cheltenham: Edward Elgar, 2010).

Chapter Four
Being Faithful in Diversity:
Beyond Exclusivism and Relativism

Being faithful in diversity. We have been considering the facts and natures of religious diversity and examining reactions to it. Now I want to explore the more difficult issue about how it is we are to be true to our religious position and live within the context of religious diversity. The challenges we face, as I pointed out, include the fact of religious diversity in itself, the decline of old supports for faith, the disappearance of former taken for granted starting places, such as the monarchy, the British empire and Christendom; and finally the rise of and presence of newer forms of inter-religious competition and conflict. Newspapers are full of images of religious conflict overseas and reports of religious competition and conflict at home. Is it possible to negotiate the competing demands and claims between religious groups and the competition and conflict between them and secularist groups? The way ahead is not simple, it is not clear and will require much effort on the parts of each and all.

The rise of experiential authority as we shift from rational to experiential criteria for assessing nearly everything, along with the rise of individualism, of a consumer society and the increasing presence of religious voices in public policy debates all combine to force us to rethink about to what it is we are supposed to be faithful in all this diversity and change. What do we hold on to as we negotiate this particular set of changes and chances in our fleeting lives? Our current situation forces us to rethink how it is we relate to others, with those who are different in belief and practice. We are forced to ask, as is every age, but now it is our turn to ask what theologies are we to use to image, motivate, assess those relationships? We are challenged to ask, how do we express ourselves in the contexts that now have multiple foundations—one of which may be ours, some of which we may understand and others may leave us just puzzled? What is our imagery for describing where we are, what are our key ideas?

I suspect that most of those who attended the lectures in New Zealand and many readers of this book, like me, come out of an old fashioned liberal Protestant background. Liberal Protestant theology and congregations were not old fashioned when I was a kid in a highly demanding conservative Calvinist denomination but were deeply liberating and affirming. However, now they seem to have become aged and old fashioned, again like me. Liberal theology was minimal in its demands. It formed a substantial and normal part of the background culture in the early to mid twentieth century, and was committed to the value of each person who was seen as a creature of God to be endowed with basic human rights. This biblically grounded and theologically well-argued orientation was critically associated with movements of liberation and peace.

Today liberal theology does not seem to generate much interest or enthusiasm. I have used the term 'low temperature' to refer to Australian spirituality, meaning that it is not dead, but that it registers rather further down the religiosity thermometer than say American religiosity. There is not very much excitement and enthusiastic religious forms are deeply suspect. Moreover Australians and many New Zealanders are also inarticulate about their faith. In part this is due to the fact that they have not been forced to speak in public from the value and theological base provided by their religious heritage whether evangelical, conservative, charismatic or liberal in theology. Indeed some liberal Protestants had presumed that to speak out of a more general, secular background which liberal theology had inspired and infected was enough to make their case and carry the day. Unfortunately liberalism is elderly. It was once dominant but is no more and now has become undetectable in policy discourse because it is either inarticulate—unable to make a scriptural and or a theological case for advancing the human condition, or is lost in secularity. Liberal Protestants now seem to fit into the expectation that religion was to be personal, peripheral, undemanding, a part of the background. However, now it is not part of much in either the foreground or the background that is changing. The mantle of religiously motivated engagement in the public sphere and in policy debates seems, for Christians to have passed to evangelicals and conservatives.

This chapter explores the challenges raised by diversity which are made more complex by the lack of a single unifying values base and considers some of the criteria that are emerging as people reject absolutism and exclusivism on the one hand and open slather relativism on the other.

Relating to Those Who are Religiously Different

The rise of religious diversity is a major marker of the primary forms of social and cultural change in the early twenty first century. The cultural and political hegemony of the British Empire has past and with it any sense of the dominance of the matters and views Anglican. We are not only aware of, but sense palpably the rise of Pentecostals, diverse spiritualities, Muslims, Buddhists, Hindus, pagans and others. We have examined the issues of incorporating religious difference into a society and have reviewed some of the challenges of religious diversity to the formation of effective and just social and public policy. There are also challenges to the way we organise our lives in this new environment and the rise of 'Christian' voices that demand policies others of us may oppose. So one of the issues raised by the very existence of religious diversity is how are we to relate to those who differ from us religiously.

Because religious difference has become more apparent and can no longer be expected to go away any time soon we have to consider and become articulate about how we relate to others. The 'we' I presume here is that of a compassionate, reflective and concerned Christian. Hard-line exclusivists have declared their approach, but that is not mine. Is there another way? There are some very conflicted approaches to how we approach others in this context of diversity. We have to admit that there are profound differences in the way that we do relate to others and we need to examine those differences as well. So not only is there difference out there, there is a lot of difference about how we approach diversity.

We have come out of a century of ecumenism. A critical issue that emerged in the efforts of twentieth century ecumenism is, 'Do we focus on things shared or things that are different?' Each of these starting points winds up in a very different place. If you focus on what is shared, you can say, 'Oh we share this sort of thing', for example, a meditative practice, or a concern for social justice, or deep respect for nature, or a practice of mystical wonder, or careful reading of sacred texts. In this approach, once similarities have been discovered and acknowledged, the rest is just non-essential details that get in the way. However, it does not take long before you stumble over those details.

Thus, when exploring similarities we must also ask, how similar are our similarities? You may think that a particular belief or practice of yours is similar to that of another person or group, but when you delve more deeply and explore the way they other group defines it, or considers it you often quickly discover that the similarities are not so similar after all or that they sit in a very different place in the order of importance. This real-ity was made very clear to me when I read a book like *The Muslim Jesus*. It is a very enjoyable read and serious compilation of the various theological and Kur'anic statements about Jesus that Muslims hold to. 'Oh, so we both believe in Jesus and hold him as key to our faiths. That is nice.' Yes, nice, until you start reading the details and you discover, 'Oh, I did not hear that particular story that way in quite that way, when I was . . .' Or, you equate Abraham, Moses, and Jesus; but we do not. Moreover, there is enough difference within each religious group to make apparent similarities seem less important; differences that are not trivial, differences that are not mi-nor details. Just get Christians to discuss what they believe about the Mass / Eucharist / Holy Communion / Lord's Supper. So the approach to dif-ferences among religious groups that play down difference and focus on similarities necessarily raises the questions of, 'how similar are the simi-larities, and how different are the differences?' Answering these questions requires a great deal of discipline and attentive engagement between those whose differences and similarities are being considered. This task is hard enough within one religious group; it becomes more difficult when you reach out beyond that.

On the other hand if the focus is on looking at the differences, critical and insurmountable differences will quickly emerge making further com-munication difficult. But others will ask, 'Well what differences are criti-cal? And Why?' And we each have ideas about what differences are criti-cal. I think we have to be more upfront about a) what those ideas about critical difference are, b) where they come from and why the difference is so critical. I say so because we have suffered too long the problem of dif-ference denial. A great deal of twentieth century ecumenism proceeded on the basis of difference denial. Difference denial is heard behind such claims as 'Religions are really all the same.' I have not served as a religious professional in eight different protestant denominations in more than five countries to fall for that one. The differences between religions and sub-varieties of religions are real and not trivial. We have discovered that dif-ference denial does not work very well.

Faithful to What?

At the very minimum being faithful in diversity means being true to our-selves, being who we are. The very fact of religious diversity raises the need to reflect on what we believe and practice. One way of raising this question is to ask, 'To what am I to be faithful?' Until diversity is encountered this questions is often left unasked and unanswered resulting in a certain level of religious illiteracy and inarticulateness about one's own religion. Not asking it explicitly can also lead to the adoption of relatively minor matters as boundary markers. Different persons and groups make different decisions about what is core, what it is that they need to hold on to in the presence of diversity.

Creed

For some religious groups being faithful to a creed is essential. Many disputes within Christianity have been settled or demarked by a creed – The Athanasian Creed declared the official Trinitarian formulation for the Church, The Reformation spawned many creeds as groups formulated their theological positions over against each other with the Augsburg Confession for Lutherans, the Westminster Confession for Presbyterians as examples. The German Confessing Church declared its position over against Nazism in the Barmen Declaration. I was raised in a very creedal religious background, The Christian Reformed Church that grew out of a Dutch Calvinist tradition. The Heidelberg Catechism, the Belgic Confession and the Canons of Dordt were declared to be the three pillars of orthodox faith. Members and especially the clergy were required to be faithful to these standards. They formed the foundation of education in the faith, the set pattern for preaching and it seemed to me that entry to heaven was conditional on getting a more than passing grade on a test of how well you knew the fine detail of these creeds. Moreover, they were the arbiters of correct thinking and if you could square whatever it was you thought with those creeds you were probably tracking alright. An example of the contemporary use of these creeds for this purpose is provided by one of my PhD candidates who aimed to assess how a particular Calvinist missionary endeavour in Papua New Guinea was being congruent with both the local culture and true to Calvinism. It was a wonderful piece of work because he was very open and honest about what things were critical and central and he also admitted to a certain degree of failure and yet at the end the missionaries' efforts there was a worshiping Christian community which was using the Christian scriptures in a way that he thought was about right and he reckoned that their beliefs were arguably congruent with core aspects of the Calvinist creeds.

Ritual practice

Other religious groups have rituals or practices that they would nominate as that to which they must be faithful through change and in the face of diversity. Examples include, the Muslim practice of performing their prayers five times a day, the Jewish practices of keeping kosher, or regular Mass attendance for a Faithful Catholic. For major Christian groups—Catholics, the Orthodox, and many Anglicans—making sure that at least the Eucharist is regularly offered in some recognisable form is critical and defining.

Religious identity

Being faithful to a particular religious identity can be critical for some persons and groups. Being Presbyterian forever, whatever that means. Danes are very clear about their Christian identity—85% of Danish youth are confirmed as Danish Lutherans while in High School, but most never attend services other than baptisms, weddings and funerals. However, in the context of rising religious diversity in Denmark their Christian identity has taken on greater salience. A religious identity means different things in different places but some people are very tied to a particular label and find that they need to keep that going even though the forms under which that label exists change dramatically over time.

How things were

Being faithful to 'how things were' is a most telling criterion, a most exacting thing to try to be true to. However, this criterion is often heard if you listen to people complaining about the way things are now. Wanting to repeat or restore the past often trips them up as they try to live up to some image of the way things were when they were young. Remembrances of things as they were set standards and expectations by which we judge the present. When I was young, you had to get to church twenty minutes ahead of time or you were not going to have a seat, and these were big buildings holding many hundreds of people. Everybody went to church, you got there early, maybe you took some reading matter along, you had some quiet time, whatever else, but at least you had a seat for the nearly two hour service. If you did not get there on time you were out in the hall. If you did not get to the hall in time you could be out on the street.

Moreover, these were youth filled churches. Congregational singing was so powerful as to be as good at shaking buildings down as a decent earthquake. Good theological discussions were to be found in ordinary groups. These are some of my childhood images that hang around in the back of my mind and say, 'This is the way things ought to be now because that is the way things work'. Most of us have similar images from youth that hang around in the back of our minds and say, 'That is the standard, how can we achieve it, will current religious change bring back religious life back to what it used to be?' The answer, of course is, probably not, most likely not. However, being aware of those things as we approach change and being aware of how we are tripped up by those expectations set by what was it like when we, or someone else, were growing up can help to rid us of unrealistic and unrealisable expectations.

Relationship with the numinous

Or is it fidelity to an ongoing relationship with the numinous that you feed, nurture, practice over time. Like any other relationship this one too undergoes profound change, has moments of going well, moments of not going well, and dark nights of the soul. Then there are such experiences as being part of a community, held in relationships that are strong, forgiving and affirming. Is it the experiences like these that count? Experiences of being with those who share your expression of faith, share in the encounter with the numinous. Is it the experience of meditative bliss, of meditative release, of meditative inspiration that is to be sought and maintained?

Faithful to what? So when we talk about being faithful within the context of religious diversity and change, fidelity to what becomes an issue and there are many different answers. I am sure that there would be many other things that other people would put on the table. There is no single answer. And once you pick a particular approach, the choice focuses the search and discussion in a particular way that limits the consideration of other views. As a result you have to be careful and aware of the consequences of selecting one criterion and setting that as the standard because that choice will determine where the conversation goes, who gets to talk, what kind of language will be used to explore the issues, and how you deal with diversity.

Theological Orientations to Difference

There are some basic theological orientations toward religious diversity that are worth exploring and clarifying as move toward the attempt to discover criteria that lift us from relativism on the one hand and release us from absolutism on the other. These include exclusivism, successionism, inclusivism and relativism.

Exclusivism

Exclusivism is familiar to us and is quite straightforward and simple. Exclusivism declares, 'I am right, you are wrong,' 'I am going to heaven, but I am not so sure about you; you are probably going to hell'. This view claims to have the truth, the only truth, and that there cannot be more than one truth. From the perspective of exclusivism, one of us has to be right and the other wrong. The logic of exclusivism seems very compelling. Some form of exclusivism is very strong within most religious traditions. It is hard to escape it or to move far away from this view, even if you are a liberal Christian open to diversity because then you are tempted to claim that liberal Christians are right and the others are wrong. While the internal logic of exclusivism seems very strong, our experience in other parts of life give ample evidence of instances where multiple truths, multiple perspectives, multiple ways of knowing are found. The conflicting theories of light provide a wonderful example. In any case admitting to ourselves that we are prone to exclusivism may well be a more honest starting point than pretending that we are wide open and accepting of every view when in fact we are not.

Inclusivism

Inclusivism takes the view that another religion is somehow included in your own, that your religious beliefs and practices include mine in some way. Watching religious leaders make this claim can be fun to watch. For example, I really get amused when my Muslim friends point out that in their view 'Oh, it is all in the Qur'an' and sweep Christianity in and other groups in a friendly embrace because 'It is all in the Qur'an'. While I greatly prefer acceptance to rejection and appreciate the genuine acceptance offered by those who use the Qur'an in this inclusive way, I am not always comfortable with the way I am in the Qur'an, or the way I am depicted in another religion's view of my faith. Moreover, they do not usually always ask me to verify or discuss their view. On this point I also find it interesting that while we might be ready to ask followers of another religion about how they do things, what they believe, what items in their places of worship are there for, but the shoe is seldom on the other foot, who has recently asked you about how you do things. People presume to know all about Christianity. The way different groups participate in inter-religious conversations is interesting and there is some gradient in the matter of who asks whom about what. Inclusivism, it is all in the Qur'an.

In another wonderful example of inclusivism, I watched Archbishop Stylianos, Archbishop and Primate of the Greek Orthodox Church in Australia, at an inter-religious meeting in 1997 in Melbourne. He gave a plenary lecture standing on a platform, fully robed. While he spoke he kept sweeping his robe around and talking about how all are included, all are included, in his wonderfully magnificent image of Christ, the Pantocrator. Everything and everyone swept up to God in Christ. His image of Jesus was truly inclusive in that it took in Hindus and Buddhists and Muslims and even Pentecostals although he was not so sure on this point, but in the end it was all there included. Similarly Hindus are often heard to say, 'Well we have a temple that has got you in it and it has had you in it for at least 1500 years'. 'We include you, you are really one of us, you are not so different after all' say the inclusivists. There is a sense that at the end of the day a theology that is comfortable with diversity is going to have a fair amount of inclusive elements. The problem with inclusivism is that while I may feel that I can include you, the question must be asked whether my inclusion of you denies some things about you that are important to you. Am I only including the bits about you that I like? But inclusivism is more of an advance toward healthy inter-religious relations than exclusivism in that it seeks a way to be mutually respectful and cooperative.

Supersessionism

Supersessionism claims that 'What is good in your religion we have adopted in ours and the rest we chucked out as unnecessary, wrong, or outmoded'. This is what Christians often say to the Jews, referring to their scriptures as 'The OLD Testament', which is improved and needs to be read in the light of 'The NEW Testament'. Following suit, Muslims say they same thing to both Jews and Christians. Indeed Muslims say that everyone is really a Muslim, but many just do not know it. The result is that one reverts to rather than converts to Islam. Mormons say to others that while they may have some truth, God's revelation to Joseph Smith restored the church to its original purity. Forms of supersesssionism can be seen other groups who essentially say that they have taken the best from each and all religions, tossed out the bad or erroneous and that they thus offer something that supplants all that went before. I get invitations to join such groups at the rate of about one a month. They argue that if we all saw the wisdom of the way they offer, then religious conflict would be overcome and peace would return to the world. In this way supersession-ism is another form of difference denial; that is the denial of the legitimacy of difference.

Relativism

According to relativism there is no basis for choosing among religious groups, they are all equally good and bad, right and wrong. One variation on this view argues that 'at their best' all religions are equal. Another form of softened relativism asserts that religions each provide a different path up the one mountain, but they all arrive at the same place. Still another argues that the pure divine light is necessarily refracted through the lenses of different religions in order to get through to diverse humanity. Many different paths, one destination, one light and a rainbow of refractions each true to the light in its own way.

While sounding very nice and inclusive, at the end of the day rela-tivism pleases no one. The acceptance that there are different paths, that there are many forms of religion and spirituality may assist in promoting moves toward co-existence, cooperation and healthy competition in inter-religious relations. While seeming to offer a 'live and let live' way forward in inter-religious relations, relativism quickly becomes another form of difference denial. The differences among religions do not count. But that begs the question, count for what? Some would argue that the differences do indeed count regarding one's fate in the next life. We will only know the answer to that question when we get there. Or is the key point whether the differences among religions make a difference for social order, social cohesion, economic productivity, or social justice? Again we are pushed to asking, by what criteria do we make these assessments.

I am not prepared to argue for the acceptance of one or another of these approaches. I think there is an honesty in some forms of exclusiv-ism, while inclusivism usually shades quickly into a form of exclusivism.

Supecessionism actually feels like exclusivism to those being superseded. While multi-faith is a social reality, it is actually a hard place to sit in unless you have a solid social theory of the positive productivity of diversity, and, if religious, you are equipped with a well argued theology of religious diversity. That kind of thinking developed in and after Vatican II for Catholics who, while arguing confidently the Catholic position, were and are able to leave room for others, legitimate space for others, and a position which leaves decisions about the eternal efficacy of religion (and none) to God, where in my view it belongs anyway.

Some Things I Know About Religious Diversity

I propose that we start the quest for criteria by which to assess religions with some things that I know about religious diversity. First, I know that religious difference is real and that from a societal perspective diversity is okay, indeed healthy, but we will explore what it means to be okay as we go along. Second religious diversity is not going to go away, I get a new offer about every fortnight, 'Please join my new religion, if we all agree to this we'll all have peace on earth and everybody will agree and it's really nice'. I usually take a look just to see which bits they have pulled together and how they are doing religion and find quite quickly that their approach does not appeal, that I would object to this bit and we would have arguments about that bit. My capacity to squelch my critical reception of any religion would ensure that peace did not come through all of us being of one mind. Third, some treat religious diversity as a disease to be healed, something to be overcome, or a threat to be repressed. This is very much a European approach to diversity and you have to understand that Europeans have been very much affected by religious diversity and religiously motivated violence over the many years. I can understand why they would see diversity as a potential threat.

Religious diversity can also, according to European history, be a rich cultural resource. A key example of this is Andalusia in what we now call Spain, in which for a period of hundreds of years Christians, Jews and Muslims lived in harmonious association with each other producing one of the high water marks of European cultural productivity. Intriguingly, and for the time it is not surprising, the basic language of discourse was Arabic. Arabic learning which was vastly superior to anything available in Europe at that time had come across North Africa providing a rich intellectual foundation for discussion. Arabic was rich, enabled precision, it was available and for a time was the language of Christian theology. Arabic enabled the discourse amongst the three religions, the production of art and poetry and science. You can still go to Cordoba and see an incredible Mosque, as well as churches and synagogues that are from that era. This golden era fell apart when someone began to push for the end of diversity and for a particular group to be dominant. Spanish religious diversity really got clobbered with the inquisition, which worked toward the Catholicisation of all of Spain. The Spanish Inquisition remains one of the uglier moments of religious diversity management that we all cringe at.

Now Spain is recognising its diversity and it has moved to a form of State funding for religions including Islam. We have not talked about the funding of religion, but in Germany if you are a Lutheran you tick this box on the taxation form and a certain amount of your income goes to the Lutheran Church. In exchange they have to marry you, they have to bury you, they have to baptise you, you do not have to attend services but the churches will be built, maintained and kept beautiful. If you are a Catholic you tick a different box and a similar provision is made. German Muslims are saying, 'Hey cannot we have a tick box too so we can build and maintain our Mosques?' The response has been 'No, you are not a recognised religion'. That is a bit rough for about 4% of the German population. By way of contrast, Spain has provided a tick box on the taxation form for more groups than just Catholics to opt into. Spain has adopted a European model for supporting religion but they have extended it greatly, recognising the reality of religious diversity. Barcelona hosted The Parliament of the World's Religion in 2004 and used that event to promote increased understanding and acceptance of religious diversity.

In this context we have to remember that the internal differences within religious groups are often greater than the between group differences. All I have to do is mention Anglicans, Jews and Muslims, to say nothing of Presbyterians, Buddhists and Hindus to know that internal difference is always there. Moreover, some of the greatest inter-religious violence has occurred between warring factions within religious groups. Examples included: Shi'a vs Sunni conflicts, Anglican Acts of Conformity, Protestant vs Catholic conflict in Ireland and the Wars of Religion in Europe. So religious difference is real, will not go away, and cannot be overcome without increasingly unacceptable levels of repression. The question is whether religious diversity can be seen to be not just acceptable, something to be tolerated, but as a healthy condition for a society. But the minute I use the term, healthy, I beg the question of by what criteria would health be assessed.

Finally, I know that there are limits to religious tolerance, just as there are limits to multicultural diversity. No society lets anybody and everybody do anything they please in any dimension of life. No one is a thoroughgoing relativist. All freedoms are limited by responsibilities, by the needs of others, and by conventions. We do not even let people do whatever they want behind closed doors. We do not live as isolated unrelated individuals, but as members of groups, families, organisations in which we find ourselves affirmed, shaped and defined.

The distinction between public and private is as hard to draw as is the distinction between that in which the public has a legitimate interest and not. Thus relegating religion to the private sphere will not solve any of the problems raised by diversity, because the private has public consequences as has the public for the private. Yes, most of us would agree that it is desirable that we are open and respectful of others, including being understanding of their religious differences. However, none of us give our respect, or come to an understanding of others without exercising judgment. I think we have to admit to the fact that most of us are occasionally quite judgmental about other religious groups – and often of others within our own. It is healthy to admit that there are limits to our capacity to tolerate; limits to what we will permit. Whether reflect on this issue as persons or groups there will be limits to tolerance. Relativists are intolerant of all intolerance, the tolerant find relativism intolerable, and the exclusivists are comfortable only with themselves.

Criteria of Assessment

Given our incapacity to sit comfortably with relativism and simply allow any and all forms of religion and spirituality to operate within our societies, are there some criteria that are more defensible than others, that are usefully applicable in this area. That this is dangerous territory can be made quickly clear by a few examples. For example, we might agree that we could not tolerate a religion that promoted violence against humans. But then what are we to do with those that argue strenuously for capital punishment, often on a careful reading of their Scriptures. But of course we would oppose any religion that promoted violence against babies and children. If you agree, then I invite those who adopt this view to take up the matter of male circumcision with the Jews and Muslims. This is not an easy area.

In what follows I will discuss some criteria that I think have some utility, while acknowledging their shortcomings.

Seeking Objective Standards

Given that relativism is not going to find wide acceptance, are there some universal standards by which to assess religions. By what criteria are we to judge? Is it by virtue of some similarity to an ideal or standard? Such standards have been used in some forms of comparative religion analyses. Religions were compared according to some kind of standard, some kind of ideal. A review of these programs now reveals that during much of the nineteenth and twentieth centuries that standard ideal looked very much like Protestant Christianity. Catholics did not quite make it, Muslims got six out of ten marks, and pagans were beyond the pale. But even today we often judge others by our own ideal image of our own group. How much are they like us? Have Muslims had a sufficient reformation recently? We judge others by where we see them to be on some kind of ideal trajectory from early religion, which might not make it to some ideal utopian end state or other. Some anthropological approaches to religion used the approximation to an ideal rational form to assess how different religions were progressing upward in an evolutionary view of religion. Religion X is stuck at the Neanderthal stage, while another religion has progressed towards rational enlightenment. We do this because we have in our minds what an ideal religion is. Take me to your creed, take me to your holy books, take me to your leader, take me to your sacraments, take me to your rituals and if a religion does not have these features we do not know what to do with them. In the past we have even created such features so that we could classify and control them. The invention of Hinduism is a case in point. So, similarity to an ideal standard has been used as a criterion, but it begs the question of what is the ideal? What is the standard based on? And why adopt one ideal, or standard over another?

Universal values

One answer to this question is posed by those who argue that not only are there universal values, but that all religions actually teach these universal values. Can we appeal to these universal values to make our judgments religions and spiritualities. This is the enlightenment ideal, the rational ideal. A few years ago I participated in Assembly of the World Conference of Religions for Peace (now Religions for Peace) in Kyoto. It was a wonderful setting, a very stimulating meeting with lots of diversity. Well, actually, they only have eight or nine recognised religions, the rest come in under sufferance. In this context Hans Kung was extolling this Global Ethic document that he and others had compiled. They claim that these ethical principles are ancient and found in every religion. They include the following. Most basic: That 'every human must be treated humanely'; which principle they argue leads to commitments to 1). A culture of non-violence and respect for life; 2). A culture of solidarity and a just social order; 3). A culture of tolerance and a life of truthfulness and 4). A culture of equal rights and partnership between men and women.

As it stands, it is a clear declaration and a call to subscribe to them. Indeed Kung argued that each of the 2,000 delegates take these home to their church, synagogue, mosque, temple, or whatever else and get them adopted so that each religious group could judge its own internal programs according to these external, universal principles. I thought, 'Oh yeah, I am going home to the Melbourne Anglican Synod and I am going to put these on the table and say Hans Kung wants you to adopt these'. This is not the way religious groups work. He obviously had not attended a religious deliberative assembly recently. If the principles do not arise from their own beliefs, stories, people and history, they will not be accepted. Few groups, especially religious groups are willing to be held accountable to external standards.

The further problem with this approach is that what pass for universal standards or values turn out on examination not to be so universal after all. First, they are not universally held. Second, there exists no globally or universally accepted list of values. Just Google 'Universal Values' and you will quickly see what I mean. Thirdly, even if we claim to hold the same values we are unlikely to rank them in the same order, thus eliminating the universality of our value frameworks. While some treat the universality of some values as giving them greater force, there is no consistently agreed for this argument. The assertion of their universality simply becomes a way to try to coerce others into accepting and applying them. Such a claim has the same logical and ontological status as claiming them to be ordained of God, or written into the orders of nature (vz Catholic 'natural law').

Sustainability

Sustainability has become a global concern since the greater appreciation of the potential for climate change and over-use of the resources of the Earth has become increasingly apparent to all. From my experience and research I would say that all religions that have been around more than one generation teach sustainable values. Now that is true in part because if they did not they would not exist. If you do not actually promote sustainable values within a group the group is going to be gone in two or three generations at the most. While no consistent or compelling basis for universal values has been developed it is possible to argue that sustainability and sustainable values provide a desirable target, a practical focus and a way of measuring the impact of religious and spiritual beliefs and practices. While such values may be universal to organisations, cultures and societies that persist though time, that does not make them 'universal' in some superior way. I argue that they are universal because they promote sustainability. A similar argument relates to the claim that such values are healthy. The problem again resides in defining health and then demonstrating how holding certain values promote health of that sort. But once again we are looking for criteria. At least for sustainability, the ultimate criterion is survival.

Sustainable values and practices might include respect, forgiveness, work, commitment to group relationships, justice in distribution of resources, and others. Many would agree with the desirability of such values but would point out that they did not get such values from some abstract 'universal' value distributor. They would rather say that they got them at their mother's knee, or in working with their uncle, or from the teachings of this or that religion.

Consequences

In a sense the argument for sustainable values is a form of consequential ethics. Actions, beliefs, practices and groups are to be judged on the basis of their consequences for self, other, the environment and the world. I would say that some beliefs, some practices are indeed toxic, that is they are injurious to our ability to live together, or injurious to human wellbeing, either personal, social or cultural, injurious to peace and justice. But again I have slipped into presuming certain criteria. Declaring something toxic means, at least that it is opposite to, or undermining of healthy, but until you decide what health is, it is not possible to define toxicity. So is relativism the order of the day? Again, I would say no. Theologies have consequences, but to whom are they accountable? That is a very interesting question that is being raised more and more in societies around the world at this time. Yes, mutual respect and social inclusion are seen increasingly, but not universally to be desirable. We have explored sustainability. What is the consequence of your theology? Does it lead to mutual respect and inclusion?

I would like to take a particular example of a theology that I find highly problematic and that from its consequences can be shown to be toxic and undermine sustainability—Apocalyptic theology. The sort of imagery found in the Book of the prophet Daniel and the book of Revelation. Rich imagery, very compelling, frightening stuff. The basic line of argument in Apocalyptic theology is that there will be a final conflict, good versus evil, good will look like losing because after all, just look at the world, but at the end God will come in, wipe out the enemy, and good and God will prevail and the righteous live happily ever after, while the wicked will rot in hell. Now if you happen to be flying through the United States of America, I suggest you go and look at airport book stalls where you will find an entire bookcase of the Tim LaHaye novels dedicated to novel style exposition of an Apocalyptic theology. Titles include *Left Behind: A novel of Earth's Last Days, Tribulation Force; The Mark: The Beast Rules the World,* over fifty—yes, fifty—other spine chilling renditions of the imagery of the book of Revelation in novel forms that will make your hair fall out, stand up on end and curl over all at the same time. The writing taking Apocalyptic theology to an entirely new height or depth. I just can't wait for the movies!

Apocalyptic theology is that kind of exciting stuff we like—good vs evil, a sort of theological Western movie, or Dan Brown novel where the good guy wins out at the end of the story. While Western movies may have originally taken their inspiration from Christian theology, I suspect in this case the influence has run the other way. However, Apocalyptic theologies which are found in each of the Abrahamic religions preaches a very strong 'us' versus 'them' exclusivist view of the world and also dehumanises the other. They are evil, in league with Satan, they are going to be damned, they are going to be wiped out, they are going to be consigned to hell, they are going to get all this nasty stuff they well deserve because they have been doing nasty stuff to us. Of course, we never did nasty stuff to them!

One problem with Apocalyptic theologies is that they are often used to promote a hopeless cause in this 'now time' among those not being ready to wait for the 'end time'. Remember that in the gospels Jesus is reported as speaking against the Zealots in his time. They kept trying to get him onside with their intent to start a war with Rome. Nobody in their right mind in first century Palestine would start a war with Rome, but this mob did and they finally 'won', their rebellion and insurrection started a war. The consequence was simple, painful and absolute—Rome came in and violently wiped them off the map, destroying Jerusalem, the Temple and Jewish society of time and place. What was supposed to happen, according to the Zealots' Apocalyptic theology was of course that, as Rome marched in, God was supposed to notice the hapless state of the faithful and to enter the battle with divine rage and wipe out Rome and winning glory for God and God's people. It did not happen that way.

While historically interesting it is important to realise that every time this kind of theology takes hold its consequences are disastrous. From a consequential view point of view Apocalyptic theology has ruinous consequences for the peoples and societies that adopt it. There are those who work in the Middle East to promote a major conflict in the Middle East because according to their Apocalyptic theology such a conflict will trigger the end of time and will force God's hand. In addition to being toxic, it is not very good theology. There are universally negative consequences. As a result we could re-examine our own theologies to see whether lingering apocalypticism is a danger, or at least to be aware of its potential dangers. When assessed from a consequential perspective most would agree that Apocalyptic theologies need to be questioned.

Part of the appeal of Apocalyptic literature and theology is that they provide a space for fear, anger and excitement. I am not sure what the parameters of a good space for that is. There are also socio-psychological dimensions to this which are very worthwhile examining. Does, for some groups, apocalypticism provide a form of catharsis, a form of release, which is expressed entirely within the group, with no real external referent and does not lead to any external policy? It does not lead them to shape policy against particular groups and it does not lead them to relate differently to people because apocalyptics are all about some mythic place in time. I think that actually does occur. It is like video games. Yes, some video games are awful. Now, not everybody who plays violent video games goes out and murders their neighbour. On the other hand, some do. So we face the old problem of do you ban something because a few abuse it. We have not banned video games yet but we do keep studying their effects.

Other theologies with negative consequences include any theology of anger and retribution. They see God as angry. Now in my mind an angry

God is a failed God. Why would God be angry if God had not failed? But of course, these theologies do not blame God, but humans, especially some humans who have failed more than others, and they are the ones who have got God angry. I find angry God theology to be a critical diagnostic for a kind of theology that may be socially disruptive, leading to violence, productive of dehumanising images of the other, and ready to use military imagery and violent ideologies that promote the social exclusion of the other to purify the society and protect God's people. Of course, perfection remains an ever-elusive goal and revenge never works, anger never satisfies and these do not form the basis for a sustainable community. Again human hubris plays a significant role in any theology that claims to know who God hates, to know the mind of the 'Almighty'. Examples of angry God theology include the Puritans who rigidly ordered their lives out of fear for an angry God. Angry God theology burned witches, started Crusades, and legitimated the torture of heretics. Then there is Cromwell who burned, pulled down and purified the churches of what he claimed was idolatry. Some violence perpetrated by Muslims seems to be grounded in the idea of an angry God seeking justice. We can examine these theologies within a short frame and see how they are negative in their consequences.

Compassion

One critical criterion that is gaining currency at the moment is Compassion. Karen Armstrong and others have produced a well-framed call to all religious groups called *The Charter For Compassion* (http://charterforcompassion.org/share/the-charter/). Because of its currency I quote it below.

The Charter For Compassion

The principle of compassion lies at the heart of all religious, ethical and spiritual traditions, calling us always to treat all others as we wish to be treated ourselves. Compassion impels us to work tirelessly to alleviate the suffering of our fellow creatures, to dethrone ourselves from the centre of our world and put another there, and to honour the inviolable sanctity of every single human being, treating everybody, without exception, with absolute justice, equity and respect.

It is also necessary in both public and private life to refrain consistently and empathically from inflicting pain. To act or speak violently out of spite, chauvinism, or self-interest, to impoverish, exploit or deny basic rights to anybody, and to incite hatred by denigrating others—even our enemies—is a denial of our common humanity. We acknowledge that we have failed to live compassionately and that some have even increased the sum of human misery in the name of religion.

We therefore call upon all men and women:

- to restore compassion to the centre of morality and religion
- to return to the ancient principle that any interpretation of scripture that breeds violence, hatred or disdain is illegitimate
- to ensure that youth are given accurate and respectful information about other traditions, religions and cultures
- to encourage a positive appreciation of cultural and religious diversity
- to cultivate an informed empathy with the suffering of all human beings—even those regarded as enemies.

We urgently need to make compassion a clear, luminous and dynamic force in our polarized world. Rooted in a principled determination to transcend selfishness, compassion can break down political, dogmatic, ideological and religious boundaries. Born of our deep interdependence, compassion is essential to human relationships and to a fulfilled humanity. It is the path to enlightenment, and indispensible to the creation of a just economy and a peaceful global community.

Armstrong puts forward the criterion of compassion. Does this theology, this policy, this program produce compassion? The theme of compassion can be seen to run through the course of theologies in most religious traditions. In many it can be seen to be held in tension, or to be the ideal counter to themes of purity and legalism. Certainly we Christians can find compassion promoted by Jesus as the corrective to legalism and ritual purity. Compassion stands in direct opposition to those patterns described in the previous chapter as competitive purity. Indeed, the message of Jesus in the gospels might lead to competitive compassion, as hearers are told to 'do unto others, as you would have them do unto you'. We know about the ugliness and pain produced through competitive purity. We cringe when we hear reports of honour and purity being held to be more important than love and understanding, or when concerns to protect the interests of patriarchy come before social inclusion and justice. We cringe about those things when we see these things, and others join us.

Compassion is a fine criterion. It is readily understood, is comparatively easy to apply and is suitable at all levels of analysis. The consequences of compassion are also clear and for Christians they are enjoined as the 'fruits of the spirit'. Compassion leads to understanding, cooperation, respect and peace. Purity and legalism lead to exclusion, conflict, judgmentalism and petty rivalry. 'I'm more pure than you are', 'They are more pure than I am', 'They, are impure and not to be admitted'. Compassion builds social cohesion and productive human relationships. Puritanical judgmentalism—arrogating to self the work of God—and legalism erode human relationships and undermine social cohesion.

Compassion makes a good criterion. It will have, if used, a variety of good kinds of consequences. For Christians calling for compassion, is a call to return to and put in practice the core values promoted by and lived by Jesus. For Muslims, every Surah of the Qur'an but two begin by describing Allah as the 'most compassionate'. It is time for compassionate Christians and others to do the theological work, to put compassion at the core of their thinking and living because if that work is not done we will not get social cohesion grounded in compassion. We will get enmity, strife, intergroup hostility like we increasingly read about in Europe. Which see in the exclusionist immigration policies being promoted in so many places. Which we see in Arizona where they were shooting teenagers trying to cross the border, while complaining that employers cannot get staff for restaurants, cleaning agencies, and other jobs. I hope the use of compassion as a criterion increases. To make this happen the whole voice of compassion needs clear theological grounding, it needs a carefully elaborated motivational framework. That is, its claim to be used as a criterion has to be established, promoted and if it finds acceptance structures of enforcement need to be designed and put into place. The likelihood of compassion or any other criterion to overcome diversity is not great.

Eternal consequences

So far we have been seeking some kind of ideal external agreed standard by which to assess the this-worldly consequence of religious beliefs and

practices. But, what about the other-worldly consequences? Eternal consequences? For example, compassion may be great for a society, but does
it get you to heaven or not? Now if matters of the next world are very important to a person or group, then this-worldly criteria take a lower priority than consequences for eternity. To be effective as criteria consequences
for eternity require belief in a life after death, the existence of different
states in that life, that admission to them is conditional, and that these
conditions are known. There have been periods of history when the issue
of eternal outcome was considered of paramount importance. It is also
interesting to observe how the conditions of admission vary from time to
time and from one religious group to another. While concern for eternal
outcomes do not seem to be predominant in most Western societies now,
as judged from current opinion polls which indicate that most people in a
places like Australia, New Zealand, Canada, Britain, and the United States
believe in heaven, fewer believe in hell and an increasing proportion believe in reincarnation. By the way, there has been a steadily rising belief
in reincarnation in formerly Christian societies. I do not know why, but
it is there. While declining in proportion, no society appears to be without those who take the life to come seriously. For them the consequences
of beliefs and behaviours in this life have significant consequences and
provide criteria for assessing other the beliefs and practices of others as
well as a basis for evaluating social policies. Such beliefs also provided the
basis for these groups to do things to others that are deemed to be good
for their eternal souls. Those who do not share these beliefs do not accept
this imposition.

Thus, there are those who claim to have objective, externally validated
criteria for the assessment of all aspects of life. The fact that the use of consequences for the next life as a criterion for assessing beliefs, behaviours
and policies cannot be proven to be valid until we get there, or do not,
is irrelevant to those who believe they are valid. If you are among those
who believe that you do know what is to come, and that God has made
the criteria clear, and maybe even appointed you the judge—although this
is contrary to scripture—then the consequences for the next life may be
more important to you than anything other consideration. Like it or not,
agree with it or not, I think we have to respect this position as one among
the many in the religious diversity that makes up our society. We have to
respect views, such as these, as providing for some people a value base for
operating in this context. What is no longer acceptable in most societies is
the imposition on others of policies and programmes, which are ground-

ed in beliefs about otherworldly consequences. These issues are real to the people who raise them, are to be respected as matters of importance to them and can be debated theologically, or scripturally; but they have little traction beyond those who believe in the same way as those who raise them. In public policy discourses such arguments should be made by those who hold these beliefs and should be recognised by others and respected by others as being very important to this group. To refuse to hear the argument is to demean and devalue one of the many voices. On the other hand, to give such views a higher order priority than other considerations is not fair to those who do not hold them. In a working civil society each group has a voice, a right to be heard, but not to override others.

The Problem of Accountability

The application of any criterion requires a system of accountability. Without accountability and enforcement, criteria have no teeth, remain pious ideals, something you might consider when all else is done. When the issue of accountability is raised, the question of 'who' is accountable to whom and for what, quickly surfaces. As does, 'who' is going to do the accounting? To 'whom' is any theology, or religious group accountable, whether it is our own, some other religious group? Making various aspects of society accountable to some body, some tribunal, some standard has been a very major part of the process of civilisation where the rights of the minority, the less powerful, the disenfranchised are defended against the powerful. In a civilised society no group has the right or unrestricted power to push others around.

Christianity, particularly in its Christendom form associated with the power of empires, was accustomed to calling others to account and ready to do that quite quickly. It gave or withheld its blessing to kings, programmes, and policies. The criteria varied, the most primary being what was seen to be good for the church. It also used the power of the state to impose its views and to enforce attendance at its services. However, Christianity in almost any of its forms is not itself accustomed to being accountable, and certainly not accustomed to the levels of transparency required for accountability. The church gets very uncomfortable when light is shone upon its operations, its decisions, or its leaders. After all, they are accountable only to God. Some of its Protestant forms are a little bit more open to accountability and transparency but they too usually have hidden behind veils of obfuscation and impenetrable bureaucracy when asked to be accountable. When I raise issues of accountability and transparency with the bishops that I know they quickly go onto some other topic. The cases of child abuse only makes this pattern of avoidance painfully apparent within the Catholic Church which still wriggles and tries to blame the victims and not accept that they need to be accountable. But it is not alone. The use of money in religious organisations is not entirely clear. The whole business of how appointments are made is less than transparent. Then there is the impact of particular teachings. For example, how much traditional teaching out of Genesis, promoting 'dominion over the world', rather than 'stewardship of God given resources' has led to environmental degradation? To what extent does the continued condemnation of same sex relations contribute to feelings of exclusion, depression and to youth suicide? It appears that the pope is beginning to confront the consequences of the Catholic Church's stance against condom use for the spread of HIV/AIDS.

But to whom are we accountable? I have been raising this issue within a Christian framework. This is complex enough. Accountability and transparency raise issues that would be just as true for other religious communities within their theological and ethical frameworks. However, hard as it is to talk about accountability within a particular religious framework, now that we live in the reality of religious diversity, the issue of to 'whom' are these diverse groups accountable becomes even more complex. Is accountability limited to their own members, to their own adherents, to their own tribunals? At one level the answer is, 'Yes'. For Christians, that was one of the particularly important moves within the Reformation, to bring in transparent structures where members had some ways of bringing clergy and hierarchy into accountability.

Religious diversity makes all of this more complex. Can one religion ever be held accountable by another religion? This question is as pertinent within religious groups as between them. For example, is it the job of liberal Christians to call other Christians into account? And if so, on what basis, since the two groups are likely to start from very different theological and scriptural positions? Nonetheless, sub-varieties of Christianity seem quite ready to be critical of each other and to hold each other to account. Is it possible to bring to account some other philosophy, or ideology? There are certainly philosophies out there, ones that feel quite comfortable judging religious groups according to their standards. Can this be turned around? Can it work at all?

To whom are we accountable? In some sense it can be argued that each group within it, is accountable to the society of which they are a part. Perhaps. But then the question becomes, what are the mechanisms of doing this accounting? The 'court' of public opinion is a powerful force. Issues of accountability and transparency are at one level handled by the negative sanctions encountered by those who violate the accepted norms of a society in free flowing forms of civic accountability where the public might say, 'Hey, that's too far, come back in'. For example, even the pope has finally bowed to pressure and has permitted the use of condoms for the prevention of disease, but not for contraception. The move of popular opinion and practice finally forced the Anglican Church to recognise divorce, stop rejecting divorced persons and permit the remarriage of divorced persons, including clergy. The reaction of public opinion has often worked to dampen enthusiasm for religiously motivated violence. However, public opinion can be quite variable and at times needs leadership and legislation to enable change in directions of greater inclusion and equity. Public opinion in some places supports the execution of blasphemers, while in others promotes blasphemy as entertainment.

Societies also bring groups to account through legislation. That should be simple, no problem, just legislate that all groups must adhere to certain principles, for example that they be transparent in their dealings—like any corporation, and not undermine the social order. Most of these laws are already in place in most societies. Why is the compliance of religious groups still and issue? On the other hand, do we really want to have legislation, like, 'Thou shalt be compassionate?' Laws already exist making illegal many forms of uncompassionate behaviour. However, using laws to promote compassion is problematic: law and compassion tend to be counter poised one leading to legalism and casuistry and the other to freer forms of caring interaction.

In addition to raising issues about the nature and effects of legislation, questions of accountability that are being re-examined now have to do with the age old issue of how religions and the state relate. Few relationships are more complex, and the catch phrase, 'separation of church (religion) and state', points less to a single form of relationship than it does to the widest variation imaginable. As states are becoming aware of some of the problems that religious diversity raises and trying to bring in legal and other kinds of structures to make religious groups accountable, some agree while others who feel their position is being undermined and their privileges removed, protest against this intrusion into their affairs. Some societies carefully regulate religion, permitting one or only a few to operate. Some legislate against conversion. Others have 'official' religions that are state supported. Others, like Australia do not regulate religion.\

That some religious groups in Australia have had a privileged and protected position is evidenced by the way they are exempted from human rights legislation and taxation legislation. In this context, some religious groups arguing from the protections provided by human rights documents regarding 'Freedom of Religion and Belief' are insisting that they are in fact not accountable, that this freedom of religion and belief gives them the right to discriminate in employment and service provision, and frees them from the provision of the religious anti-vilification act in Victoria. They provide various theological and sociological arguments for their position as they seek to be able to act in ways that would certainly counter the criterion of compassion, but are in accordance with religious beliefs they hold. How is a society to respect both the freedom of religion and belief and the rights of its citizens to health social and educational services without discrimination and to live their lives without being vilified? While the answer may be obvious to some, it is not to me.

There are ways that the state is being called on to provide the court in which issues related to religious groups and inter-group relations are handled. The separation between ecclesiastical and secular courts has not always been clear. Both New Zealand and Australian courts have heard heresy trials. Australian courts were appealed to over changes to the Anglican *Book of Common Prayer*. While often viewed with some awkwardness by the courts, cases are heard and adjudicated according to the law. For example, the Exclusive Brethren were recently convicted in a Victorian court of violating the anti-discrimination act by refusing to rent a facility to a homosexual group. A small fine was payable. Cases involving religious vilification have been heard with highly contested results.

But there are times when the issues go beyond the boundaries of a state. Is there some independent body, like the 'World Religion Court', to which you might refer some religious group for promoting whatever you thought was harming you or other group? I do not know, but these are very real issues. Whatever, there is a strong call for religions to be made accountable in some way. So who can call a religious group to account and for what, by what means, are serious issues facing societies at this time.

An Alternative to Judging

The search for external, objective and universally agreed criteria has failed to produce any such thing. The raising of criteria keeps alive and feeds an orientation of judging self and other. Judging comes so very easily to us. Many have been raised in environments where every one and every thing is subject to scrutiny and judgment. Is there an alternative? But, does being faithful to ourselves, being who we are require judging others as lesser, inadequate or in error? One alternative to judging is dialogue. This alternative actually requires us to move beyond judgmentalism, beyond the application of criteria, not to relativism but to a grounded and fluid dynamic of conversation that includes religious and other groups. Groups involved in discussions in which both positive and negative things can be said. The aim of dialogue is to learn about the other, to appreciate and to clarify your own position, and where possible to arrive at an agreed course of action. It is not to convert, not to change, but to develop the capacity to work together by having an ongoing conversation that includes everyone where you can say, 'Hey look, what about that?', 'Are you sure you want to do that?' 'Are you sure that is the way you want to take your theology, philosophy, or whatever?'

In a larger conversation all voices come in, and they get heard. For example I have been part of a team conducting community consultations on issues related to the 'Freedom of Religion and Belief' in Australia. Most of these consultations were open to all religious groups. Each representative of a religious group had to take their place along side others and express their views. A few were conducted for a limited Christian group organised by the Australian Christian Lobby. In these groups the like-minded played off each other as though there were no other views and escalated in their condemnation of those not present. In the open forums the conversation early on made it clear that there existed very real differences that could not readily be solved or reduced to non-existence by the views of another group. In one consultation there was somebody from the rationalist group, an active atheist, and he said, 'Why don't you just keep it all at home, keep it private'. The response of other people in the room came in the form of pointing out that they had to say, 'No', because 'our faith requires this', or 'our faith motivates us to do that', etc. This response was put in a confident but dialogic sort of way. To which the rationalist said, 'Oh, I can now see why you can not just kept it private'. Now there was also a move on the other side saying, 'Ah, okay but we agree with this stuff over here and think that it is an issue'. 'Yes, oh we can work with you on that'.

So a conversation occurred that included a diversity of people and people in that conversation were challenged to express their own position. Each learned from the other and moved beyond stereotypes and quick fix solutions to their differences.

There are many forms of dialogue. One typology proposes four types: head, hands, heart and soul. In 'head' dialogue we discuss each other's theology, beliefs and practices as objective realities. Often done with literature or videos about the other. The other may not even be present. In 'hand' dialogue we work together on some project. 'Habitat for Humanity' has been very successful in bringing highly diverse people together to build low cost housing for the poor in many parts of the world. In the process of working together stereotypes are abandoned, past animosities and ignorance are overcome and with the sense of mutual accomplishment comes a sense of inclusion. 'Heart' dialogue involves trying to understand each other's religious experience. This involves a great deal of exposure to the practices of the other, asking and listening to learn what things mean and what effects are experienced. In 'soul' dialogue there is the attempt to worship together.

The first three types of dialogue are very important to coming to understand and appreciate another religion. Books alone are not enough. I do not think we really understand how Buddhism works for a Buddhist, or how Judaism works for a Jew, or how something else works for somebody else unless we deeply engage with them. As far as being able to worship together, I give up. I am not even sure that this is an ideal. It is so highly problematic. My favourite story along this line is, somebody was proposing an inter-faith worship service and said, 'Surely we can be silent together', and one of my favourite Jews put up his hand and said, 'No, no Jew is silent before G-d, Jews argue with and rage against the almighty'. That ended the search for a common form of worship. I was pleased someone had the courage to refuse to be included.

In the context of this conversation of dialogue, you have to be able to say who you are and in doing that you will clarify your position and you will learn about others as they clarify theirs and that is so refreshing, so refreshing. If you have the opportunity to actually do it and I have done it with several groups, 'What do you like about your religion?', and each person says. These are religious diversities. 'What don't you like about your religion at this time?', and each person goes around and states them. Now, you can ask questions among each other but they had been revealing what was important, what was precious, what was questionable and when they had become that human they were able to really learn more about each other in a very deep and meaningful kind of way. But it caused the outcomes, yes, respect, articulate, confident, discerning, compassionate, better understanding of how the group handles issues but to do it you have to respect, you have to listen, you have to state your own position and that is one of the most critical things for liberal Protestants; to have to say something.

I gave the example of my wife taking Anglicans to Mosques and then saying to the Anglicans, 'and the Muslims are coming to visit us'. Upon hearing this these Anglicans just went white with anxiety saying, 'What are we going to say? They are going to ask us about our faith.' However, when asked about their faith they found answers and came away more richly understanding of themselves as Anglicans, richly understanding of Muslims and ready to work together and putting judgment aside, understanding how the other group worked. Neither group watered down who they were, nor pretended to be what they were not. Each group became more confident in who they are, clearer about their beliefs and practices and more comfortable to be who they are religiously.

The role of confidence is so terribly important in inter-religious relations. If you are confident you can communicate with others easily. But if you are not confident you will feel uncertain, ill at ease, and quickly become fearful and distrustful. You might even blame the other for making you feel that way and become angry. Dialogue is an incredible process but it is totally different to judging. Dialogue does not worry about criteria; it aims to get to know the other, to develop an understanding. Not everybody can do it, not every group is willing. It is a process into which people can be invited. I have even watched some pretty strident evangelicals, either of the atheist sort or of the Christian sort, temper, become part of the group and ready to move forward, which is why I am very happy to invest energy in inter-religious relations and dialogue.

Is Dialogue the Answer?

However hard we work at it dialogue is not all going to lead to peace and nirvana. Careful articulation of views and respectful listening may simply clarify a very strong point of disagreement. Dialogue like marriage counseling may result in greater understanding and even reconciliation, but it is also likely to result in increasingly clarified differences which will not go away no matter how good willed the participants. I have found this to be the case regularly in my dealings with Evangelical Christians. I am happy to talk with them, I am happy to declare my position although I get pretty wary because I know how it will be used. And it does sharpen the difference and I go away saying, 'We are different and on that point we disagree'.

The management of such internal diversity can be very taxing. Just ask the Archbishop of Canterbury. When inter-religious dialogue moves beyond sharing cups of tea it is very likely that differences will emerge that are simply are not going to be easy. These may involve differences in belief, or about social policy. We might be able to agree to do something together, like respond to a crisis, building a house for the poor, feeding the hungry, or providing medical help. But there are other issues that will divide. Issues such as provision of abortion, condoms, same sex marriage, will generate a lot of steam and we will not come to agreement. However, I would rather get to the realisation of disagreement through a respectful conversation that involves the people who were being talked about, who face the issues, and whose lives will be affected by our decisions. I find that preferable to an ideological and theological stone throwing fest.

The Perspective of Diversity

Thus at the end of our search for criteria, for an independent and objective set of standards by which to assess religious beliefs, actions and hopes we return to where we started. We cannot escape or overcome diversity. Diversity is not only the reality we face, it also characterises the varieties of responses to diversity including all those attempts to overcome it through appeals to reason, higher order principles, structures and law. At the end of the day we are different as persons, we live in different communities, we are shaped by different cultures. Difference is all pervasive along with a degree of shared humanity. No basis of agreement prevails without feeling coercive to some. We live in a community of communities, a world of difference.

For some in this context of diversity, being faithful in diversity means being a person of faith along side of others, making and sharing space for others, being a person of a particular faith, knowing it, enjoying it, being articulate about it and its implications to others. In this context societies will hold groups and persons accountable according to established legal frameworks. In this context groups will contest for influence through formal and informal means. Some will be more open to diversity than others, but that is part of the diversity. From the contestation will emerge tentative, partial and imperfect solutions to the problems of life. Given the known costs of repressive forms of overcoming diversity the likely trend will be to accommodation and inclusion. However, no society is free of those who seem willing to pay these costs and demand that they be paid. Being faithful in diversity means that we take responsibility for being who we are as persons and as religious groups in a context of diversity, ready to stand, ready to articulate our position, ready to listen and allow other voices to be heard and ready to be accountable.

Some Further Reading

Armstrong, Karen *Charter for Compassion.* Accessed 22 November 2010 http://charterforcompassion.org/site/

Audi, Robert and Nicholas Wolterstorff, *Religion in the Public Square: The Place of Religious Convictions in Political Debate* (New York: Rowan and Littlefield, 1997).

Bouma, Gary, Rod Ling and Doug Pratt, *Religious Diversity in Southeast Asia and the Pacific: National Case Studies* (Dordrecht: Springer, 2010).

Fenn, Richard, *Dreams of Glory: The Sources of Apocalyptic Terror* (Burlington VT: Ashgate, 2006).

James, Helen (editor) *Civil Society, Religion and Global Governance: Paradigms of power and persuasion* (London: Routledge, 2007).

Kung, Hans 1993 *Declaration Toward a Global Ethic.* Accessed 19 December 2010 at http://www.weltethos.org/pdf_decl/Decl_english.pdf.

Lyons, Jonathan, *The House of Wisdom: How the Arabs Tranformed Western Civilization* (New York: Bloomsbury, 2009).

Khalidi, Tarif (editor) *The Muslim Jesus: Sayings and Stories in Islamic Literature* (Cambridge MA: Harvard University Press, 2001).

Sykes, Helen (editor) *Future Justice* (Sydney: Future Leaders, 2010).

Theimann, Ronald, *Religion in Public Life: a Dilemma for Democracy* (Washington DC: George Washington University Press, 1996).

Wollterstorff, Nicholas, 'Why we should reject what liberalism tells us about speaking and acting in public for religious reasons', in Paul Weithman (editor) *Religion and Contemporary Liberalism* (Notre Dame: University of Notre Dame Press, 1997), 162–81.

Chapter Five
A Way Forward

Diversity is a fact, an unavoidable fact in the daily lives of each of us. Efforts to overcome diversity through some imposed uniformity of race, ethnicity, culture, or religion are doomed to fail. In advanced modern societies social cohesion depends not on similarity, not on being alike, but on the realisation that we need each other. Religious groups and communities are not dispensable or irrelevant to civic life. Highly differentiated urban societies thrive on and depend on diversity to develop creative solutions to the challenges of sustainability, productivity and communication. They also demand that the diverse groups within them work together to produce what is needed from minerals and food to organisations and culture. This diversity is not a disease to be overcome, nor is it a passing moment on the way to a new singularity, a new culture, or a new order. Given these facts and the fact that where we fail to cooperate, where we engage in conflict, societies stagger, fail to produce and reproduce; we need theologies affirming diversity, we need to change our orientations to diversity welcoming it as healthy and desirable, indeed something to be nurtured and treasured.

We have seen that compelling, seemingly objective criteria are only found within a given framework to which some, but not all persons or groups are already committed. Thus, some bewail the rise of individualism, or the passing of solid foundations, but this appears to be where we recognise our situation. A theological case could be made that we live in a sort of grey zone, or is it a rainbow, which enables freedom of the will and responsibility of persons and groups—the situation into which God places us and into which God risks God's self. But such a case again can only be made within a particular committed framework, one with which I am familiar and use regularly. I also recognise its limitations both as a framework for understanding my life and for capturing the whole of God. But then nothing ever does. Given that we each as persons and groups ground our ethics in such necessarily limited bases and that no overarching sacred canopy, compelling moral order is available today, nor likely to be developed or if developed likely to find wide acceptance other than through its imposition as an ideology enforced by overweening state violence; how are we to proceed?

First, theologies of diversity need to be articulated within each tradition. Catholics are well ahead on this with the Vatican II and post Vatican II encyclicals, notably *nostra aetate,* calling for respectful interaction with other faiths. Popes John XXIII, Paul VI and John Paul II were active in respectful interactions with those of other faiths, particularly Anglicans, Orthodox, Jews and Muslims. Current Roman Catholic leadership is not as enthusiastic about these activities, but the theological foundation has been laid and can be appealed to by any Catholic seeking respectful interaction with those of other faiths.

However, for my stripe of Christians—Anglicans and Protestants—the hard theological work lies ahead. Old fashioned liberal theology is just that, old fashioned. It amounted to an Enlightenment, rationalist and highly cerebral form of Christianity and has little appeal today given the greater appeal of experiential forms of authority and spirituality. Liberal theology enjoyed its high water mark in the 1950s with Niebuhr, Tillich and Bultmann. It enjoys a sort of dead cat bounce in what is currently called Progressive Christianity, but that too is an elderly form of Protestantism and subject to all the problems of rationalism—too cerebral and verbal. Meanwhile, conservative Protestants seemed locked into an exclusivist approach to diversity. Pentecostalism is more open to some forms of diversity, but has not relied on the Spirit to release them from bondage to biblical literalism and exclusivism. While these groups have the younger people they have yet to develop the theological skills needed to grapple positively with diversity, but some probably will in the near future.

For those Protestants who take their Bibles seriously and who wish to begin the project of building a theology of diversity it is possible to start with creation and its rich diversity, the ways diversity is essential to life and the problems that emerge from the repression of diversity. God looked at creation and all its diversity and called it 'good'. I find great delight and comfort in God's response to the Tower of Babel—diversity, 'there is not one way to God'. Then there is the theological discussion Jesus has with the Samaritan woman at the well, which has nothing to do with 'husbands' but with ideas about whether the Jerusalem Temple was the only place to worship God. Again the response is to affirm diversity. For a taste of the development of these ideas see (http://www.youtube.com/p/ F80971249C2A59FB?hl=en_US&fs=1) or Google 'Bouma St Michaels'. And this is but a start of the rich trove of material available for this work to those who work in this committed framework.

Second, rather than throwing around charges of relativism, developing respect for the ways existing moral frameworks work would be a better starting point. Yes, each will provide detectably different ways forward, define different end-points as ideal and prescribe different paths to achieve the ideal. Each will satisfy some and not all. There will be conflicting views about life, death, sexuality, justice, the nature of the 'given' order, and which forms of self-sacrifice are necessary, healthy, or unnatural and perverted. The reality that diversity is a given and not singularity, and that each of these moral frames has been around for a long time suggests that no one of them is likely to be demonstrably better on all counts than another mean that some form of respect is in order both to understand and to see how they each operate to support sustainable human communities.

Third, respectful dialogue is needed to come to an understanding of different strands of religious diversity. This is true both within religious traditions and between them. Judging another to defective or demonic without careful listening prejudices the capacity to understand and appreciate. Such dialogue will reveal points of similarity and agreement, but it will also reveal insuperable incompatibilities, differences in starting points, differences in the ranking of importance of one factor or another. The understanding emerging from respectful dialogue will clarify both agreement and disagreement, but the way these belief and ethical frameworks operate will be understood by all parties in the discussion. To facilitate respectful dialogue places of discourse need to be designed, offered and used. Civil society is supposed to be such a place, but is not at the moment structured in a way to promote this sort of discourse. Some religious groups have facilitated dialogue in good faith and have provided examples of ways forward. There are now many organizations that promote interreligious understanding and harmony at local, national and global levels. Ideally a legislative assembly would be such a place, but our current parliaments, senates, and houses of representatives bear a problematic resemblance to a place of respectful discourse.

In all of this, a new appreciation of the givenness of diversity will become increasingly assumed. As we have come to appreciate the necessity and health of biodiversity so we may come to appreciate the value of cultural and religious diversity for healthy societies. Increasing there will be an appreciation of the good features of diversity. These will be seen along-side the challenges, problems and perplexities posed by diversity. Accept-ing the givenness of diversity and finding ways to affirm and celebrate it seem to be far healthier approaches than any attempt to overcome it, to wipe it out, or to impose uniformity. Doing this still requires fundamental change in our assumptions about diversity, a letting go of our fear of and resistance to change, and a new openness to the future. But the cessation of change is death. Life is a process of continuous change. Each religion and spirituality provides a foundation for hope and techniques for incul-cating, celebrating and applying a faith in the future grounded in an un-derstanding of the past and the now.

Gary D Bouma
Epiphany 2011

Index

Accountability, 97-98

Apocalyptic theologies, 91, 92

Atheist, 1, 5, 6, 10, 13, 19, 37, 41, 64, 101, 103

Anglican, 1, 6, 7, 8, 10, 12, 13, 15, 18, 26, 31, 32, 38, 42, 54, 60, 70, 71,77, 80, 86, 89, 99, 100, 103, 108

Boundaries, 25, 26, 32, 38, 39, 40, 31, 44, 94, 100

Buddhist, 4, 8, 9, 14, 17, 27, 43, 53, 54, 56, 60, 64, 77, 83, 86, 102

Canada, xiv, 1, 7, 8, 12, 13, 15, 18, 23, 26, 31, 47, 55, 56, 96

Catholic, 4, 6, 7, 8, 9, 10, 12, 13, 14, 15, 16, 22, 31, 32, 33, 35, 41, 50, 53, 54, 55, 56, 57, 58, 62, 69, 80, 85, 86, 88, 89, 98, 108

Christian
    Nation, 14, 54
    Society, 14, 60, 69

Christianity, xii, 4, 9, 10, 13, 19, 21, 30, 37, 38, 50, 64, 67, 79, 82, 83, 88, 97, 98, 108

Compassion, xii, 16, 18, 25, 30, 37, 57, 62, 63, 64, 65, 66, 77, 93, 94, 95, 96, 99, 100, 103

Competition, 25, 26, 32, 34, 36, 40, 43, 47, 53, 55, 58, 75, 84

Competitive Piety, 36, 37

Conflict, 1, 15, 16, 20, 25, 26, 29, 31,32, 33, 34, 35, 36, 37, 38, 39, 43, 44, 45, 48, 50, 52, 53, 54, 58, 68, 75, 77, 82, 84, 86, 91, 95, 107, 109,

Congregations, 76

Consequences
    Eternal, 95–96

Criteria, xiii, 75, 76, 82, 84, 85, 87, 88, 90, 96, 97, 101, 103, 104, 107

Dehumanisation, 38, 41, 42

Demography, 10, 13

Dialogue, 64, 71, 101, 102, 103, 104, 109

Discrimination, 42, 53, 100

Exclusivism, 72, 75-106, 108

Freedom of Religion, 15, 61, 100, 101

Globalisation, 4, 26

Homosexual, 40, 41, 100

Identity, 2, 5, 10, 16, 18–21, 31, 40, 80–81

Inclusion
    Strategies of, 70–72

Inclusivism, 82–83, 84

Islam, xii, 4, 6, 11, 20, 21, 32, 33, 37, 38, 40, 42, 46, 55, 57, 59, 63, 65, 84, 86

Interdependence, 51, 52, 73, 94

Jews, xii, 9, 10, 56, 71, 73, 83, 85, 86, 88, 102, 108

Legislation, 21, 29, 30, 35, 38, 41, 42, 43, 45, 59, 66, 99, 100

Marginality, 26

Market place, 21

Mormons, 4, 61, 84

Muslim, 4, 8, 9, 11, 13, 14, 15, 17, 19, 20, 27, 32, 33, 36, 38, 40, 42, 43, 49, 50, 53, 55, 56, 57, 59, 60, 61, 62, 63, 65, 70, 71, 72, 73, 77, 78, 80, 82, 83, 85, 86, 88, 93.95, 103, 106, 108

Nation, 2, 3, 7, 8, 9, 11, 13, 14, 15, 21, 22, 27, 38, 52, 53, 54, 56, 59, 61, 63, 67, 71, 109

New Zealand, ix, x1, x11, xiv, 1, 3, 4, 5, 7, 8, 9, 13, 14, 15, 16, 17, 20, 23, 25, 26, 27, 29, 30, 31, 38, 47, 49, 50, 53, 55, 56, 57, 59, 61, 62, 63, 64, 65, 66, 67, 70, 76, 96, 100

Objective standards, 88

Pagans, 41, 77, 88

Parishes, 13

Peace of Westphalia, 2, 41, 54

Pentecostal, 4, 7, 10, 11, 12, 14, 27, 34, 41, 42, 77, 83, 108

Policy, 1, 15, 16, 18, 19, 22, 47, 48, 50, 54, 61, 62, 63, 67, 68, 71, 75, 76, 77, 92, 94, 97, 104

Presbyterian, 6, 7, 8, 10, 12, 14, 18, 26, 27, 31, 38, 39, 50, 54, 66, 79, 80, 86

Progressive Christianity, 4, 108

Protestant
        British, 12, 29, 31

Public discourse, 27, 62

Relativism, xiii, 75, 76, 82, 84, 87, 88, 91, 101, 109

Revitalisation, 1, 16, 26, 27, 28, 29, 30

Rhetoric, 33, 34, 42, 57

Rights, xiv, 16, 17, 18, 41, 42, 66, 76, 89, 94, 97, 100

Same sex, 29, 41,64, 98, 104

Secular, 15, 21, 22, 23, 27, 30, 35, 37, 61, 62, 66, 70, 75, 76, 100

Secularism, 22, 70

Social Cohesion, xiii, 2, 3,14, 47, 48, 49, 50, 51, 52, 53, 54, 55, 56, 58, 59, 67, 68, 72, 73, 74, 84, 95, 107

Spirituality, xiv, 4, 5, 13, 14, 21, 22, 23, 28, 29, 61, 76, 84, 87, 110

State, 2, 3, 14, 21, 22, 30, 34, 36, 38, 39, 53, 54, 55, 59, 60, 61, 66, 69, 88, 92, 97, 99, 100, 108

Supersessionism, 83, 84

Sustainability, 2, 68, 90, 91, 107

Tolerance, ix, 2, 21, 87, 89

Values, 16, 27, 34, 35, 36, 45, 48, 49, 64, 65, 67
        Christian, 64
        Core, 3, 41, 95
        Dominant, 3
        Religious, 65, 67, 72,76, 89, 90,
        Sustainable, 90

Universal, 64, 65, 66, 88–90

Vilification, 38, 41, 42, 43, 59, 100

Violence, 1, 2, 22, 33, 34, 37, 42, 43, 44, 46, 47, 53, 55, 57, 58, 63, 68, 85, 86, 87, 89, 93, 94, 99, 108